Ireland's
Mammals

Juanita Browne

Published in 2005 by
Juanita Browne,
Browne Books, Calverstown, Kilcullen, Co Kildare, Ireland
00353 (0) 86 3442140

www.irishwildlife.ie

Text and Design © Juanita Browne
Images © photographers/illustrator

Printed in Belgium by Proost

ISBN 0-9550594-0-2

A catalogue record for this book is available from the British Library

AN ROINN COMHSHAOIL, OIDHREACHTA AGUS RIALTAIS ÁITIÚIL
DEPARTMENT OF THE ENVIRONMENT, HERITAGE
AND LOCAL GOVERNMENT

This publication has received support from the
Department of the Environment, Heritage and Local Government

SUPPORTED BY THE HERITAGE COUNCIL

LE CUIDIÚ AN CHOMHAIRLE OIDHREACHTA

This publication has received support from the Heritage
Council under the 2004 Publications Grants Scheme

Acknowledgements

There are so many people who have offered me encouragement and help I cannot mention them all here, but please be assured your support has not gone unnoticed.

I am particularly grateful to the photographers who responded to my idea for this book with great enthusiasm: Mike Brown, John Carey, Billy Clarke, Jacquie Cozens, Eddie Dunne, Simon Ingram, Conor Kelleher, Andrew Kelly, Vincent McGoldrick, Richard Mills, Nigel Motyer, John Murphy, Phil Richardson, Philip Smyth, Padraig Whooley and Christopher Wilson. Their photographs speak for themselves. We are all indebted to these determined artists who must brave Irish weather and often peer through an empty viewfinder for hours on end in order to capture these wonderful images of our unique wildlife.

My thanks to Sinéad O'Connor, RTE, and John Murray and Ross Bartley from Crossing the Line Films for their help in sourcing images taken during the filming of the *Wild Trials* series, and to Ray D'arcy, Carrie Crowley, Conor Lenihan, Don Wycherley and Pat Falvey for taking these photographs.

To my very talented friend, Maria Archbold, who not only provided illustrations but also translated my text into Irish; and offered so much encouragement and had so much faith.

A big thank you to those patient and kind people who were good enough to proof-read my text: Dr Tom Hayden, Dr Colin Lawton, Dr Simon Berrow; Conor Kelleher; Br Raymond McKeever; Cepa Giblin, Betty Anne Browne and Terry Donnelly.

My thanks to Isabell Smyth, Fionnuala Lynch, Dr Liam Lysaght, Michael Starrett and all at the Heritage Council. My thanks to Aisling Browne, Gareth Quill, Jonathan Stone, Judith Browne, Rosita Agnew and Ray O'Sullivan, for offering their expertise and support. A special word of thanks to Vivienne Molloy who offered constant help. To Marc Lysens, in Proost, for his professionalism and advice.

My humble thanks to Don Conroy, Michael Viney and Éanna Ní Lamhna, for agreeing to read my book and offer their thoughts. Their response to my efforts is most appreciated.

I would especially like to thank Dr Alan Craig and Peter Carvill, of the National Parks and Wildlife Service, for offering to sponsor my book, and for their enthusiasm for this project which was most reassuring to the independent publisher.

Finally, I would like to thank all my friends and family for putting up with my frequent absences over the past 18 months and for all their encouragement.

To my husband Joe for his unwavering support and love, thank you.

– Juanita Browne, Author

About this book

The aim of this book is to increase awareness of our mammalian fauna. This is a book for readers of all ages and offers an accessible introduction to Irish mammals. It introduces the reader to the life of each animal – where it lives; what it eats; when it breeds; and its adaptations for a particular lifestyle.

Each common land mammal is discussed in the Species profiles and this is complemented by an Irish language section. A sample is provided of the whale and dolphin species observed in Irish waters – the cetaceans covered were chosen in order to illustrate the diversity of life in Irish waters.

The common name, Irish name and scientific name is provided for each animal.

Average weights and body measurements are provided. It should be noted that these figures refer to the *average* size for adults of each species, though in some cases there may be much variation. These figures are courtesy of Tom Hayden and Rory Harrington, and I would direct readers to their wonderful book, *Exploring Irish Mammals*, for more detailed information on our mammals.

I hope this book offers a gentle introduction to our wildlife that will encourage further reading and a lifelong interest in our wild animals and our environment generally. A contacts list and further reading list facilitates further learning and involvement in conservation.

I hope this book causes the reader to reassess their thoughts about the Irish countryside and its wild inhabitants – that it might encourage us to see Ireland as a living landscape, with many interesting and charismatic characters.

For my father, George

Contents

Introduction

What is a mammal?

A mammal is an animal with a backbone. The female feeds its young with milk, produced by special glands called mammary glands. A mammal is able to maintain their own body heat. Their body temperature is usually higher than the temperature of their surroundings – a mammal's body temperature is usually between 32-40ºC. Because muscle and nerve action increases at higher temperatures, animals must have a certain body temperature before their bodies can be fully active. Mammals can be active no matter what the exterior temperature.

Reptiles and amphibians cannot maintain their own body temperatures. Their body temperature varies depending on the temperature outside. These animals are only fully active when external temperatures are high enough and their bodies have warmed up enough, usually to between 25-30ºC.

Mammals are usually covered with hair. Some mammals have become so adapted to living in the sea – the whales and dolphins – that they have lost most of the hair from their bodies and instead rely on blubber for insulation.

Mammals native to Europe are 'placental' mammals. This means the babies grow inside their mothers, nourished by a special organ called the

'placenta'. There are also other types of mammals – such as the marsupials, which are found in Australia and South America. Marsupials give birth to a very underdeveloped baby, sometimes only a few centimetres in size, which crawls into the mother's pouch where it grows, feeding on its mother's milk.

Depending on their diet, mammals show a range of habits and their bodies are specially adapted to the plants and animals they eat. For instance, the fox is a meat-eater so it has sharp canine teeth to help it to catch fast-moving prey. Mammals that graze on grasses have wide flat surfaces on their cheek teeth for grinding down plants. They also have a special stomach with a number of chambers to help them digest plant material. Rodents have large incisors for gnawing on their food – seeds and nuts – and rodents usually don't have any canines as they don't need canines to catch live prey.

Most mammals are found on land and walk on four legs, but many show a variety of adaptations. They have evolved to live in very different conditions. Through evolution, some mammals that live in water have legs that have developed into 'paddles' to help them swim more efficiently and quickly. Others, such as rodents, are excellent climbers and burrowers and can squeeze through very small spaces. Bats are mammals that have evolved

What is a mammal? You are a mammal.

over many thousands of years to be able to fly. So, we see a lot of variety in mammals. Otters have webbed feet to help them swim. Their bodies and limbs show modifications that help their lifestyle. The ability of mammals to adapt to different environments makes them very successful animals.

Dogs, pigs and cats are mammals. Other domestic animals are also mammals, such as cows, horses, sheep and donkeys.

Mammals come in all shapes and sizes. The African elephant, cheetah and gorilla are 'mammals'. They have backbones made up of vertebrae; and they give birth to live young which are fed by their mother's milk

Mammals around the world

Mammals are found all over the world. There are 4,680 different mammal species. Almost 200 mammal species are found in Europe. Mammals in Ireland range in size from the tiny 4g pipistrelle bat to the grey seal, weighing in at 240kg. The largest animal to have ever lived on the planet, the blue whale, can reach up to 30 metres in length and can weigh over 100 tonnes. The blue whale is known to cruise along the west coast of Ireland. The smallest mammal on Earth is the Kitti's hog-nosed bat, which weighs only 1.5g, 100 million times less than the blue whale!

The earliest known mammals were tiny creatures that looked like shrews. They lived 210 million years ago. It was from one group of these animals that all mammals evolved, including man. About 60 million years ago, the dinosaurs were probably wiped out after an asteroid, or a number of comets, hit the earth. After this, the mammals expanded, diversified and eventually evolved into the variety of mammals we know today.

Habitats

Mammals are found in habitats ranging from the coldest to some of the hottest places on earth. This is possible because a mammal has hair on its body and it can maintain its own body temperature. For instance, camels are large mammals that have adapted for survival in hot deserts, while polar bears patrol the frozen Arctic and seals are found hauled out on beaches in the Antarctic.

There are about 1,100 bat species flying in the world's skies, while seals, dolphins and whales can dive to great depths in our oceans.

'Habitat' is defined as the place where an animal lives and where it can find all the necessities for life. Some of our Irish mammals are associated with certain habitats – for example, squirrels are usually found in woodland areas, while the otter spends much of its time in rivers or around our coasts.

'Introduced' Species

When a species is brought, by man, from lands where it occurs naturally to lands where it has not previously lived, we refer to the animal as an 'introduced species'.

Sometimes 'introductions' of animals and plants occur accidentally, unknown to man. For example, the black rat spread from Asia to countries throughout Europe by climbing aboard ships and hitching a ride. The American mink was brought to Ireland to be bred on Irish fur farms, but many escaped from these farms and now live in the wild. Descendants of these animals are now found throughout the country.

Other animals are introduced by man on purpose – for farming (e.g. rabbit) or for other economic reasons or to control pests. Some introduced species can have a negative impact on a country's wildlife and upset the natural balance. For example, the grey squirrel was introduced into Ireland in 1911. It is native to North America, but people believed it would make a good addition to the Irish fauna, so they released some grey squirrels in Co. Longford. However, the grey squirrel is now spreading throughout the country and this spread seems to be related to a decline in our native red squirrel, which may soon face extinction in Ireland.

The hippopotamus is adapted for life in water.

Scientific Names

Zoologists are scientists who study animals. Zoologists give all animals scientific names to avoid confusion. This is because an animal could have many different common names, and different names in different languages. For example, we have an animal in Ireland called the stoat, but many Irish people have traditionally called this animal a 'weasel'. While there is an animal called a weasel in Britain, it does not live in Ireland. To avoid confusion, zoologists use the name 'Mustela erminea' for the stoat, and this is recognised by other scientists all around the world, no matter what language they speak.

Scientific names also show when animals are related to each other. For example, the stoat, *Mustela erminea*, belongs to the same 'genus' as the American mink, *Mustela vison*, which tells us they are similar in some way or they share a common ancestor.

Scientists group animals, plants, bacteria and fungi according to physical similarities and common ancestors, giving us an evolutionary tree stretching back millions of years.

This 'classification' of animals is changing all the time as zoologists learn more about how different species are related to each other – by studying the body structure, bones and teeth; by looking at fossils; doing field research; and by looking at the genetic similarities of different groups.

All living things are put into groups to show how they are related to each other:

A kingdom consists of related phyla.
A phylum consists of related subphyla.
A subphylum is made up of related classes.
A class is made up of related subclasses.
A subclass is made up of related orders.
An order is made up of related families.
A family is made up of related genera.
A genus is made up of related species.

Here is an example of this classification:

Classifying the Irish mountain hare
KINGDOM: **Animalia** – Living, multi-celled things that are not plants, bacteria or fungi.
PHYLUM: **Chordata** – Animals with stiffening rods along their backs.
SUBPHYLUM: **Vertebrata** – Chordates with backbones made up of vertebrae.
CLASS: **Mammalia** – Vertebrates which produce milk to feed their young.
SUBCLASS: **Placental mammals** – Mammals whose young develop inside the mother and are well-developed at birth.
ORDER: **Lagomorpha** – the hares, rabbits and pikas – small herbivores (plant-eating animals) with large incisors in the upper and lower jaws, and small peg-like incisors behind the upper incisors. Lagomorphs can move their jaws forwards and backwards as well as from side to side as they grind up plants.
FAMILY: **Leporidae** – the hares and rabbits. There are 49 living species of hares and rabbits.
GENUS: *Lepus*
SPECIES: *timidus*

Two names are used to refer to each species. These are usually based on Latin and are always written in italics. For example, the scientific name for the mountain hare is '*Lepus timidus*'. *Lepus* is the genus it belongs to, along with other hares, such as the Brown Hare, *Lepus europaeus*. '*Lepus timidus*' makes it clear that we are talking about the species, the mountain hare. '*Lepus*' is Latin for 'hare' and '*timidus*' is Latin for 'timid', so we see its scientific name means the 'timid hare'.

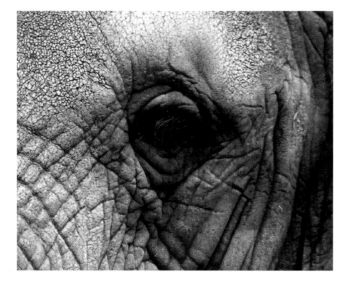

Mammals are usually covered with hair. Some need fur to keep warm. Other mammals, such as the elephant, have only a sparse covering of hair. The colour and pattern of mammals' coats are very variable, as shown by the fur on a zebra (top right). The hedgehog has spines which are special modified hairs.

The badger has special scent glands which it uses to mark its home and to communicate with other badgers

Sometimes animals of the same species begin to show differences. This can be because they are separated from others of their own species and are evolving in different habitats and conditions, living among a different combination of other animals and environmental factors. These isolated populations can become sufficiently different so that they are called 'subspecies'. The Irish mountain hare is different to the mountain hare population found in Britain (unlike the mountain hare in Britain, the Irish mountain hare does not turn white in winter). So we give it an extra piece added to its scientific name – *Lepus timidus hibernicus*. 'Hibernicus' means 'Irish' so when we hear the name *Lepus timidus hibernicus*, we know this is the Irish mountain hare.

Skin, hair and keeping warm

As mammals maintain their own body temperature, they are usually covered in hair. Some mammals have fine, tightly-packed hairs, or 'fur' which helps them to keep warm. Others have lost much of the hair from their bodies. This can happen if the animal lives in a climate where keeping warm is not so important, for example, the African elephant has only sparse hair on its body. Whales and dolphins have also lost their hair because they have evolved other ways to keep warm. Seals have thick layers of fat ('blubber') under their skin to help them stay warm. They also have short stiff guard hairs to protect their skin when they come ashore on sand and rocks.

Just as you wear different clothes in summer and in winter, animals with fur coats also need different amounts of protection from weather at different times of the year. They usually moult their coat once or twice each year. For example, in winter, the fox has a thick fur coat to help it stay warm. This is moulted at the start of the summer and is replaced by a short coat during the warmer months when it doesn't need as much heat.

Mammals that spend a lot of time in water must also keep warm. The otter has a thick layer of 'underfur', made up of millions of tiny hairs. This underfur traps air next to the skin and helps to keep the animal warm. Over this underfur the otter has long, tough 'guard hairs' that help to keep the underfur dry. In this way, the otter has a double fur coat to keep water away from its skin when it's in the water.

Communication

You may have noticed that many mammals in the wild are very quiet or silent, most of the time. This is so that they avoid being noticed by predators or prey, but many mammals do make a range of sounds, for example, barks, growls, squeaks, howls and bellows, when threatened, excited or when they are communicating with other animals.

Red deer stags roar loudly during the breeding season to warn off other males and to attract the notice of breeding females. The stags that bellow most often and for the longest time often attract the most females. This is a way for them to show their size and strength.

Mammals also use scent to communicate with each other. Many mammals have special scent glands which they use to mark their homes – to communicate with other animals that this area is occupied. Scent also tells other animals if an animal is in breeding condition and whether it is male or female.

Mammals can often move each ear independently – this helps them to hear predators or prey, without moving their bodies. Hearing is very important to mammals as many are active at night, when sight is less useful to them. Many animals can detect ultrasonic sounds, high-pitched sounds too high for human ears to detect. Some use ultrasonic sounds to communicate. Mice communicate with their young using ultrasonic sounds.

Echolocation

Bats have the most highly developed hearing of all mammals and they use their hearing more than their sense of sight. Bats hunt using 'echoes'. They emit ultrasonic sounds and the echoes made as these soundwaves bounce off objects help them to navigate and to locate prey. This is how a flying bat can catch a tiny insect, such as a midge, in complete darkness – it makes high pitched sounds and listens out for the returning echoes as they bounce back from the midge's body.

Most bats make these sounds through their clenched teeth and most have large ears to help them hear the smallest echoes. While humans can't hear these high-pitched sounds, they can be detected using special machines called 'bat-detectors'.

The horseshoe bat emits sound through its special nostrils. It has a special fold on its nose, which is horseshoe-shaped. This flap of skin helps to direct its ultrasonic sounds.

Whales and dolphins also use echolocation to help them navigate through the ocean and to help them find food.

Nocturnal animals

Many animals are 'nocturnal' – this means they are most active at night. They feed and socialise with other animals after dark. Many animals have evolved nocturnal habits so that they avoid predators or because they are less likely to be caught by a predator after dark. Others hunt after dark because this is when their prey is available. For example, bats hunt night-flying insects.

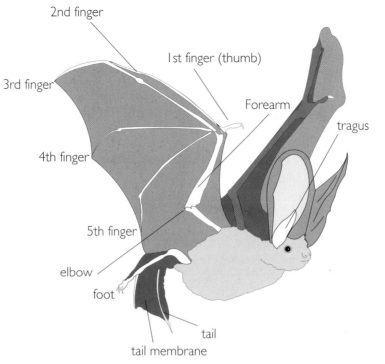

2nd finger

1st finger (thumb)

3rd finger

Forearm

tragus

4th finger

5th finger

elbow

foot

tail

tail membrane

A bat's wings are actually made of skin and the modified bones of the forearm and fingers.

Bats – life in the air

There are 1,116 bat species and new species are still being discovered. Nine bat species have been found to breed in Ireland. Irish bats are small social mammals that live on insects and spiders. They have special adaptations that allow them to 'see' using sound. They use echolocation to find their way around and to catch prey. Echolocation is a sonar system in which the bat emits very high-pitched calls and their highly developed brains and ears detect the echoes from these sounds as they bounce off objects. This use of ultrasound to see their surroundings in the darkness allows bats to catch the smallest of insects. Bats can fly at speeds of up to 50 kilometres per hour through complete darkness! The tragus, found in the ears of most bats, is a fleshy lobe used for identification of different species.

Diet

Our nine bat species have different behaviours that mean the competition for prey is reduced. Some hunt moths, others eat large insects such as beetles, while others fly low over water to pick up insects. Some hunt over open farmland areas, while others hunt in woodland.

Hibernation & Home

Our micro-bats regulate their body temperature to use less energy and survive through cold weather and times when there are few insects to feed on. When their body temperature drops and they become less active, this is called 'torpor'. Irish bats spend long periods over winter in hibernation. Bats choose roost sites in cool, humid places such as caves, hollows in trees and mines, for hibernation in the winter months. Before our forests were removed by man,

most bat roosts were probably in hollows in trees. Some bats still use trees, but others have adapted to using sites in buildings, under bridges and in mines.

Breeding females choose different roost sites in which to give birth. Breeding roosts must be warm and the bats often huddle close together in groups to save energy spent in keeping warm. Females usually give birth to only one baby each year. Bats make up for their low reproduction rates by living a long time. A bat may live for up to 30 years in the wild.

Habits & Myths

Bats are nocturnal and are not often seen by humans. There are a lot of myths about bats, including the belief that bats are blind and fly into your hair if you meet one after dark. This is untrue. Bats are not blind and because they are able to use echolocation to find tiny insects and fly quickly between tree branches in the pitch dark, they are not likely to fly clumsily into a person's hair.

The largest bats in the world are the flying foxes. Some flying foxes have wingspans of 1.7 metres! Flying foxes feed mainly on plant material, ripe fruit, flowers, nectar and leaves.

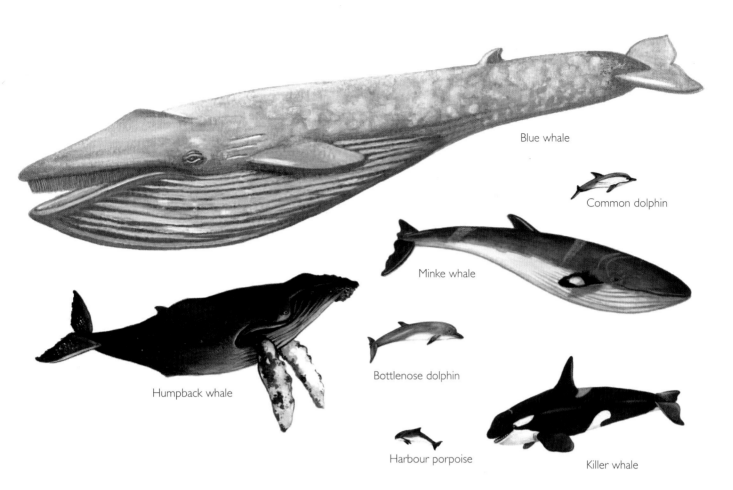

Blue whale

Common dolphin

Minke whale

Bottlenose dolphin

Humpback whale

Harbour porpoise

Killer whale

Whales and Dolphins – life in the sea

To date, 24 whale and dolphin species have been observed in Irish waters (see page 158 for a complete list). These range from the largest animal on earth, the blue whale, down to the small harbour porpoise.

In 1758, the whales and dolphins were finally recognized as mammals and not fish. Like mammals that live on land, whales and dolphins maintain their own body temperature, breathe air through their lungs and give birth to live young which the mother feeds with milk produced by its mammary glands.

Whales and dolphins evolved from land-dwelling mammals that returned to the world's oceans to feed, developed special adaptations for their environment, and eventually evolved into the animals we know today, which spend their whole lives in the sea.

Whales and dolphins lost the coat of hair seen on most land mammals. This is because a coat of hair would slow them down as they move through the water. Instead, whales and dolphins have a thick layer of blubber under their skin. This provides insulation and helps them to keep warm.

They also evolved streamlined bodies to help them move under water. The whales and dolphins belong to the Order Cetacea, so we call them 'Cetaceans'. This order is made up of the toothed whales and the baleen whales. There are 72 species of toothed whale, including small dolphins, porpoises, beaked whales, the sperm whale, killer whale, beluga and the narwhal. Toothed whales have many teeth in their jaws and feed mainly on fish and squid.

There are 13 baleen whale species. The blue whale, humpback whale, minke whale and fin whale are baleen whales. Baleen whales have special horny plates – called 'baleen' – in their jaws instead of teeth. They use the baleen plates to strain or filter tiny plankton and larger invertebrates, as well as small fish, from the water.

Many whales and dolphins can dive to great depths. The sperm whale can dive as deep as 3,000 metres to feed!

The largest animal to have ever lived on the planet, the blue whale, can reach up to 30 metres in length and can weigh over 100 tonnes. A mammal this size could not live on land. Its limbs would have to be so huge that it would not be very mobile. In water, its body weight is supported and it has a streamlined body.

Scientists believe that whales and dolphins may be closely related to the Artiodactyla, even-toed ungulates, which include our deer and goats. It may have been from animals like these that whales and dolphins evolved!

Nigel Motyer

You can tell the wood mouse
from the house mouse by its
larger eyes and ears.

Wood Mouse

Luch (luchóg) fhéir
Apodemus sylvaticus

Body length: 9-10cm
Tail length: 9cm
Weight: Males 20-27g; females 17-24g

The wood mouse is a pretty rodent with large eyes and ears, and a long tail. Its fur is chestnut-brown on its back and head, and light grey underneath. It usually has a small yellow patch on the front of its neck, and its snout is covered in long sensitive whiskers. Unlike the house mouse, the wood mouse does not give off a strong smell. It has large hind feet, about 2cm in length, which it uses to leap into the air if frightened.

Habitat & Home

The wood mouse is found throughout Ireland; in gardens, hedgerows, parks, on sand dunes, farmland, blanket bog, woodlands and grasslands.

The wood mouse prefers cover, so in fields where the grass is short, the wood mouse usually sticks to the edges, where it can forage in undergrowth. It is unusual for wood mice to enter buildings. Wood mice are nocturnal and spend the daytime underground, in large burrow systems.

Diet

Wood mice eat seeds, grains, berries, acorns, mushrooms, buds and bulbs, as well as small invertebrates such as larvae, snails, and earthworms. They use the same pathways each night as they forage for food and will store food underground in their burrows or in other holes or old birds' nests. Each night, a male wood mouse travels over an area about half the size of a football pitch as it searches for food.

Over winter, when the weather is cold, a wood mouse can enter a sort of 'torpor', when its body temperature drops by a few degrees. This helps it to conserve its energy and survive through times when food is scarce.

Breeding

Breeding usually takes place between April and October. Gestation (pregnancy) lasts for about three weeks and the mother gives birth to four or five babies, which are blind and furless at birth. They are weaned after only three weeks, and the mother might become pregnant again very quickly. Mice are very successful breeders and produce many young each year.

Wood mice rarely survive more than a year in the wild. They are hunted by barn owls, long-eared owls, kestrels, badgers, pine martens, foxes and stoats. Therefore the wood mouse is important to many other animals as they rely on it for food.

Bank vole

Luch rua / Vól bruaigh
Clethrionomys glareolus

Body length: 10cm
Tail length: 5cm
Weight: Males 25g; females 22g

The bank vole was first discovered in Ireland in Co Kerry in 1964. It was probably introduced to Ireland accidentally by man some years earlier. It is now found throughout Munster and has spread into Galway and Leinster.

The bank vole has a short body and blunt face. Its chubby body makes it look a bit like a hamster, so it is easy to tell the bank vole from the wood mouse. It has small eyes and ears and a shorter tail than a mouse. It has a reddish brown coat that is grey on its belly. The bank vole has a very good sense of smell and special scent glands it uses to mark its territory.

Habitat & Home

Bank voles like to move about under cover so they usually live in woodlands, scrub or hedgerows, where there are plenty of plants close to the ground. They are 'diurnal', which means they are active during the day, but they usually feed at dawn and dusk. They make nests above ground and in underground burrows, which they line with leaves, grass and moss.

Diet

Bank voles eat plants, berries, seeds, nuts, fruits, fungi, insects, larvae, earthworms and snails. They often take food underground to eat it in safety or to store it for later. They sometimes strip the bark from young trees to reach the layers below the bark. Bank voles can climb well and may climb into the lower branches of a hedgerow in search of food.

Breeding

Breeding usually takes place between April and October, and after a gestation (pregnancy) of about three weeks, the young are born. The mother gives birth to a litter of between one and seven pups, which are blind and naked when born. The mother communicates with its young by using little high-pitched squeaks, sounds that are are too high for humans to hear. They are fed on their mother's milk until they are about three weeks old. Then they leave their mother to find their own territories. Most bank voles don't live longer than about a year and a half in the wild. Bank voles are important in the diet of foxes, stoats, pine martens, barn owls and other birds of prey in the south west of the country where they are found.

House mouse

Luch thí

Mus (musculus) domesticus

Body length: 7-9cm
Tail length: 7-8.5cm
Weight: Males 13-25g; females 14-30g

The house mouse probably arrived in Europe hidden on the boats of early human settlers, and has been found in high numbers here since the 7th century. The house mouse's coat is grey-brown in colour; its underside is paler. Its tail is long and scaly and its coat is greasy like that of a rat. Unlike other mice, the house mouse gives off a strong smell. Females are a little larger than males. Its eyes, ears and hind feet are smaller than those of the wood mouse.

Habitat & Home

The house mouse is common throughout Ireland. It got its name because it likes to live in human dwellings, including outhouses, farm buildings and industrial buildings, especially through winter. It is also found in hedgerows and fields close to buildings, but most people will see the house mouse from the corner of their eye, as it darts across a room in their house. It runs along the edges of the room and around furniture because it doesn't like crossing open areas. This is because small mammals know they are more vulnerable in the open – they are more likely to be caught by a predator in the open, especially if a bird of prey is watching.

In buildings, house mice live under floorboards, in wall cavities or ceilings. If your house has mice, the squeaks you hear are probably the sounds made by mice quarrelling over territories. The house mouse is mainly nocturnal and uses the same pathways each night as it looks for food. When it lives outdoors, it digs large burrow systems where the ground is soft.

Diet

The house mouse will eat almost anything, including glue, plastic and soap, if they can't find anything tastier. It gnaws at wood and at the plastic insulation on electric cables. It has to gnaw on hard surfaces to wear down its front teeth, which grow all the time. Outdoors it eats cereals, insects and larvae. Indoors humans provide a wide range of foods for the house mouse to enjoy!

Breeding

Breeding occurs all year round if the conditions are good – if the female has access to enough food, shelter, mates, etc. Outdoors, it usually breeds between April and

Billy Clarke

The house mouse's tail is about the same length as its head and body.

October. A pregnant female builds a nest using any material she can find, including shredded paper, material or grass. After a gestation period of three to four weeks, a litter of four to 10 pups are born. Young mice are called 'pups'. They communicate with their mothers by high-frequency squeaks that humans can't hear. Even though they are born with no fur and blind, they grow very quickly and are weaned when they are only 16 days old.

Many birds of prey and mammals, such as the barn owl, kestrel, stoat and fox, feed on the house mouse. House mice living indoors fare much better in cold weather than wood mice living outside and many survive more than two years.

If conditions are good, one female could give birth to ten litters in a year, so numbers can increase very quickly. Mice thrive on human wastefulness, so they have become very successful survivors. Like rats, house mice are seen as pests as they contaminate food and carry disease.

House mice are excellent climbers, and can jump and swim very well. (*Mus domesticus*)

Black rat

Francach dubh

Rattus rattus

Body length: 20cm
Tail length: 23cm
Weight: Males 160-250g; females 130-190g

The black rat was once common in Ireland but declined after the arrival of the larger brown rat, early 18th century.

The black rat is also known as the 'ship rat' because it used to be common on ships and it spread to new countries in this way.

The black rat can climb well and can run down mooring lines from ships to reach new land. Despite its name, its coat colour varies from brown to black, and it has a grey belly. It is smaller and weighs less than the brown rat and has a sharper face, with long whiskers and larger eyes and ears. It also has a longer, thinner tail than the brown rat. Its tail is often longer than its body.

Zoologists believe the black rat has been in Ireland since at least the 9th century, and became common here in the 12th century. The black rat probably first appeared in tropical Asia and spread into Europe as humans travelled back and forth to India and Egypt.

The black rat is associated with the Black Death, which caused the deaths of 25 million people in Europe in the 14th century! The bacterium that caused the disease was carried by fleas found on black rats.

Black rats in Ireland went into decline after the arrival of the larger brown rat. The black rat evolved in the tropics, so it is less used to cold weather and less adaptable than the brown rat. Many black rats were poisoned around shipping ports in the 20th century and modern ships are built differently – so it is not as easy for the rats to climb aboard.

The larger, more aggressive brown rat is now found all over Ireland and on many offshore islands, while the black rat may be extinct on the mainland. It may still be found on Lambay Island, off Dublin's coast, as bones of a black rat were discovered on the island in 1988.

Eddie Dunne

A brown rat runs away with a tasty piece of sausage! (*Rattus norvegicus*)

Brown rat

Francach donn
Rattus norvegicus

Body length: 22-28cm
Tail length: approx. 20cm
Weight: Males 270-500g; females 250-400g

The brown rat arrived in Ireland from Asia in the early 1700s. It came ashore from trading ships. It can climb and swim well so the animal had no problem getting ashore, by climbing down mooring ropes from the boats.

The brown rat's upper body is grey-brown and paler underneath. Sometimes they are completely black in colour and can be mistaken for the black rat, which is a smaller animal and is extremely rare or absent from Ireland. It has a long scaly tail and a pointed snout. The brown rat has excellent hearing and a well-developed sense of smell. Like other nocturnal mammals, they see very well in low light conditions. They have lots of whiskers and long tactile hairs on their body, which help them to find their way about in complete darkness using touch. Zoologists have found that rats also memorise their surroundings to help them find their way in darkness. They use the same pathways every night.

Because rats are used in laboratory experiments and are kept as pets, we probably know more about this mammal than any other. Laboratory rats are specially bred strains of brown rats; they don't give off a strong smell and are tame compared to their wild cousins.

Habitat & Home

Most people dislike rats because they are associated with disease and many live in places that humans would find disgusting, such as rubbish tips and sewers. They have evolved so that they thrive on man's wastefulness. Rats will live anywhere they can find food and shelter – on farms, city streets, industrial and commercial premises.

In good weather, brown rats often live outside in hedgerows and among arable crops. They excavate dens in complex underground tunnel systems in banks or hedgerows. In late autumn, as the weather worsens, rats shelter in buildings and outhouses.

Habits

All rodents must wear down their front teeth because they grow constantly. They do this by gnawing – often on woodwork, pipes, and electric cables, which can sometimes cause short circuits and fires. They consume and spoil large amounts of animal feed and stored grain, and many carry diseases. The brown rat, like other rats, has greasy fur, so you may see dark stains around indoor rat holes and along attic beams, where a rat's coat has rubbed against the surface.

The brown rat has strong senses of hearing and smell. This fellow has climbed a tree to get to nuts in this bird feeder.

Brown rats are an important prey item to predators such as barn owls, buzzards, foxes, and stoats. In fact, brown rats are the most common item in the barn owl's diet. Therefore, these predators, such as barn owls, are important to man as they keep rat populations under control. Farmers are now beginning to understand the importance of encouraging barn owls to nest on their land and some even construct nest boxes for the birds in the hope that they will help control pest populations.

Brown rats are social animals and will live together in groups, where a 'social hierarchy' develops, with dominant and subordinate animals. They spend time grooming each other and will fight off and sometimes kill rats from other clans that enter their territory. Brown rats usually feed at night but will be seen during the day if food is available. Young or subordinate rats are sometimes forced to forage during daylight to avoid competition with dominant animals.

Diet

Rats will eat almost anything, including cereals, seeds, root crops, earthworms, snails, birds' eggs, silage, bones, fruit, and even dead animals they come across. They usually carry food away to a safe place before eating it.

The brown rat can climb well. It has a long scaly tail covered with hairs.

The brown rat's coat can vary from light to dark. This is a young juvenile.

Breeding

Rats reproduce very successfully. A single female can give birth to five litters of three to 10 pups each year. Most litters are born between March and November in large nests built by the females. Pregnancy lasts for three to four weeks. Pups are naked and blind at birth. Mothers use ultrasound, high-frequency squeaks, to communicate with young. Pups are fed by their mother for three weeks before emerging from the burrow. Only 10% of brown rats survive to their second year.

Eddie Dunne

Red Squirrel

Iora rua

Sciurus vulgaris

Body length: 22cm; tail length: 18cm
Weight: male 250-390g; female 240-350g

The red squirrel has been found in Ireland for many thousands of years, since before the last ice age, but it died out a number of times. The removal of native woodlands helped to cause its decline. It was reintroduced in the 19th century from British populations. The red squirrel has again become rare in Ireland since the arrival of the grey squirrel in 1911 and may not be found today in areas along the west and north coasts. We are not sure how the presence of the grey squirrel affects the red squirrel but the red squirrel's decline has occurred at the same time as the increase and spread of the grey squirrel. Some zoologists believe that because the grey squirrel eats a more varied diet and can eat seeds before they are fully ripe, it may be able to survive in more varied habitats than the red.

The red squirrel is smaller than the grey squirrel. Its coat is brown to red in colour. Its belly is cream. In summer, the coat is lighter in colour and the ear tufts are small and pale. In winter, the coat gets thicker and redder in colour and the tail is bushier. The ear tufts get longer and thicker and make the ears look very long and pointed.

Squirrels use their sense of touch to help them find their way about. They have special sensory hairs on their face, legs, feet, tail and belly. They also have very good eyesight and a good sense of smell. They use special scent glands in their mouths and their urine to mark their homes.

Chris Wilson

A squirrel can run up and down a tree trunk very quickly. It can leap from branch to branch using its tail for balance. Squirrels are also good swimmers!

Billy Clarke

Diet

The red squirrel likes to live in coniferous woodland, including Scots pine woods, where they can eat plenty of cone seeds, pollen, buds and shoots. They also eat berries, beech mast, fungi, fruit and nuts.

Habitat & Home

Red squirrels are found in a variety of habitats where they can find enough food to eat, including broadleaf woods, parks, mixed forests and coniferous woods. They spend most of their time high up in the trees. Grey squirrels, on the other hand, spend more time on the ground.

Squirrels are diurnal, meaning they are active during the day – usually in the morning and before nightfall. During winter, they don't spend as much time out and about looking for food so that they can save energy during cold weather. Squirrels do not hibernate through winter; instead they store up extra food in hiding places on the ground. They bury nuts in lots of different places and may hide thousands of pieces of food towards the end of summer. In winter, these food stores help the animal survive through times when food is scarce. Sometimes the squirrel doesn't collect all their food stores and lost seeds produce new trees.

The red squirrel builds a nest called a 'drey' in a tree. They use twigs and bark to make the rounded nest, which they line with leaves and grass. Each squirrel may have a number of dreys. They sometimes make nests in hollows in trees.

Nigel Motyer

Like all animals that live in trees, the red squirrel has very good eyesight. Its eyes are located on the sides of its head.
This squirrel has climbed down to the woodland floor to collect food from a hiding spot.

Breeding

Breeding occurs between December and September. A female usually produces one litter each year, occasionally two. The number of litters depends on how healthy she is and how much food is available. Males fight for access to females.

The young are usually born in summer, between May and August, after a gestation period of about seven weeks. Three to six young are born in the drey. They are blind and have no fur at birth. The mother returns to the drey to feed her young for nine weeks, until they are weaned. Young squirrels may stay with their mother until she has her next litter. Only one in five young squirrels survive to their first winter. Successful adults may survive for two to six years.

Nigel Motyer

Grey Squirrel

Iora glas
Sciurus carolinensis

Body length: 26cm; tail length: 22cm
Weight: male 440-650g; female 400-720g

The grey squirrel comes from the deciduous woods of the eastern United States and Canada. A number of grey squirrels were released in Longford in 1911 and the animal is now found in 20 counties to the east of Ireland, and it will probably spread throughout the country. It is quickly becoming our most common squirrel and is replacing our native red squirrel, which is in danger of extinction in many parts of the country. The grey squirrel is bigger and heavier than the red squirrel. The grey squirrel has a brownish grey coat. In summer the fur on its back can look reddish. The belly is white.

This agile grey squirrel tries to steal nuts from a bird feeder.

Eddie Dunne

Grey squirrels are now common in Irish gardens and parks, where they are often fed by visitors, like this one photographed in St. Anne's Park in Clontarf, Dublin

Squirrels have good senses of touch, smell and sight. They use secretions from special glands in the mouth and their urine to mark points around their homes. Squirrels have special sensory hairs on their face and body to help them 'feel' their way. This helps them to leap from branch to branch as they move through their woodland home. They run up and down trees stretching out their tails for balance. Grey squirrels are diurnal (active during the day) and spend a lot of time on the ground.

Habitat & Home

Grey squirrels usually feed on seeds from broadleaf trees so they are found in Irish broadleaf and mixed woods, hedgerows, parks and gardens. Squirrels build large spherical nests called 'dreys' using twigs and bark. They line the inside of the drey with leaves, grass and moss. They may use a number of dreys in their home range. In summer they use open dreys, like platforms in the tree, but in winter, the dreys are enclosed and spherical in shape to provide more shelter.

The grey squirrel produces special enzymes that can detoxify acorns, making them safe to eat – this may make them more successful than the native red squirrel. The grey squirrel has very short ear tufts, while the red squirrel's ear tufts are long and fluffy.

Diet

Grey squirrels have a broad diet, including seeds, flowers, and fruit. They like beech mast, hazelnuts, pine cones, and acorns from oak trees. Because grey squirrels spend a lot of time foraging for food on the ground, they sometimes find food stores hidden by red squirrels. During summer they spend more time in the treetops as they search for food. Grey squirrels are clever animals that will raid vegetable patches, root crops, orchards and bird feeders. They strip bark from broadleaf trees to reach the sugar-rich sap underneath.

Breeding

Breeding occurs between December and July. Males may fight for access to females. Females produce one or two litters each year, one in spring and one in summer. After a gestation period of about six weeks, three to seven young are born furless and blind in a drey. They will be weaned when they are about 10 weeks old. A grey squirrel will be lucky to survive three years in the wild; in fact most do not survive their first winter.

Hedgehog

Gráinneog
Erinaceus europaeus

Length: 25cm
Weight: Male 900g; female 600g

Everyone knows what a hedgehog looks like. It's difficult to mistake it for anything else. The Irish name 'gráinneog' means the 'horrible one', but most people agree that hedgehogs are one of our cutest animals.

The adult hedgehog is about 25cm long and has over 5,000 hard spines on its back. When threatened, it rolls itself into a ball and the spines protect it from most predators, except perhaps from a determined badger or a hungry fox. It has coarse hair on its face and belly. Although they're difficult to see, hedgehogs do have quite long legs and can run quite quickly when they have to. They also have short tails, about 2cm in length. Hedgehogs have a good sense of smell and good hearing, though their eyesight is poor.

Habitat & Home
Hedgehogs are found in broadleaf woodlands, gardens, meadows and hedgerows. A hedgehog may wander for three kilometres each night as they search for food! They usually have a few different sleeping nests in the area where they live and forage for food. They are most active after dark, but young or sick animals are sometimes seen during daylight hours. They rustle through leaf litter looking for slugs and other invertebrates, snorting and snuffling as they go. Unfortunately many hedgehogs are killed on our roads so this is when most people see them. They probably roll into a ball when they sense the danger, but their spines are no match for a car.

Diet
Hedgehogs mainly eat caterpillars, beetles and earthworms, but will also make a meal of slugs, snails, earwigs, millipedes, birds' eggs, small mammals and even dead animals they may come across. They also eat fruits and berries.
Gardeners should welcome hedgehogs into their gardens because they feed on slugs and snails, which eat the gardeners' plants.

Hibernation

In winter, these food sources decrease so the hedgehog has a clever way to survive. It hibernates. This means they enter a sort of deep sleep so that they use less energy and can live off their fat reserves until spring. During hibernation, the hedgehog's body temperature drops to the temperature of its surroundings and its heart rate slows from over 150 beats per minute to about 20 per minute.

In October or November, they find a quiet sheltered spot and build a hibernation nest using grass and leaves. They don't stay asleep all winter, but wake up once in a while to urinate or sometimes to move to a new nest. Hedgehogs emerge from hibernation in March or April, depending on the weather.

Breeding

Hedgehogs breed between May and October and most young are born in early summer, after a gestation (pregnancy) period of about five weeks. The female gives birth to three to five young in a nest in June or July. The young are covered in a thin

The hedgehog's spines are really modified hairs. They are dark brown with white tips. The spines are very sharp and measure about 25mm. Each one can be moved separately and can be raised for defence when the hedgehog feels threatened. Each spine drops out after about a year and a new one grows in its place.

The hedgehog rolls itself into a ball when threatened and its tough spines protect it from predators.

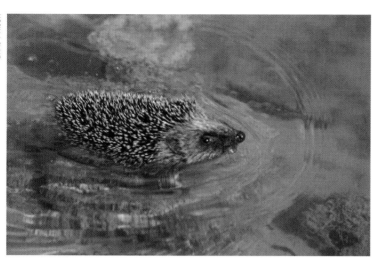

Although they're difficult to see, hedgehogs do have relatively long legs and can run and swim well.

skin when born, so that their sparse white spines don't hurt the mother. They are very vulnerable at this stage as they are blind and can't roll into a ball and have fewer spines than the adults. After just two weeks, their eyes open and many brown spines have grown on their backs. When the young are a month old, the mother leads them out of their nest to forage each night. They are now able to eat solid food instead of just drinking their mother's milk. When they are just six weeks old they are independent and already have about 2,000 spines to help protect them from predators. Many hedgehogs don't survive their first winter. The average lifespan for a wild hedgehog is three years, but some may live longer.

Conservation tips

It is very important not to disturb hedgehogs or other animals such as bats or frogs during hibernation. They can waste energy when they are disturbed and can die from stress. It is also extremely important not to disturb hedgehog mothers in the days just after they have given birth as they may abandon the nest.

Some people offer their local hedgehogs a saucer of milk and bread, but while they'll love it and lap it up, this is not good for them and the milk can give them diarrhoea. If you want to offer food to a hedgehog in your garden, it's much better to leave out some tinned petfood as this is closer to their natural diet.

Interesting Facts

Hedgehogs are famous for their fleas as their spines can hide large numbers, but don't worry – these fleas are only interested in hedgehogs and are harmless to humans or other animals.

Sometimes white hedgehogs are found. Usually a white or 'albino' animal is very vulnerable to attack from predators because they stand out so much from their surroundings, but this isn't the case with white hedgehogs – white spines work just as well as brown ones!

Pygmy Shrew

Dallóg fhraoigh
Sorex minutus

Billy Clarke

Length: Body: 4-6cm;
tail 3-5cm
Weight: 5-6g

The pygmy shrew is Ireland's smallest mammal, weighing in at only 3g in winter when their food sources are low. Breeding adults weigh between 5 and 6g.

The pygmy shrew's body is covered in short thick brownish fur. Its belly is lighter in colour. In autumn it grows a longer winter coat of fur to protect it from the cold. This is moulted in late spring to reveal their short summer coat.

The pygmy shrew has small eyes, which is probably why their Irish name 'Dallóg Fraoigh' means 'the blind animal of the heather'. It has a long pointed snout with long whiskers that twitch as it searches through leaf litter for food. They use their senses of touch, smell and sound more than their sight. They may be small but pygmy shrews can swim and climb well.

Habitat & Home

The pygmy shrew is common all over Ireland where there is good ground cover. It likes grassland and hedgerows, woodlands, and bogs. Pygmy shrews tend to use the same pathways as they look for food. They use dried grass to build spherical nests under ground cover, rocks or dead wood. Though they don't dig burrows, they sometimes use the burrows of other small mammals.

Pygmy shrews are very territorial. They will not tolerate other pygmy shrews coming into their territory and will fight if necessary. They hiss at each other and make high-pitched squeaks.

Diet

Pygmy shrews have to keep very busy in order to survive. Because they are so small they lose body heat more quickly than a larger animal (due to weight to surface ratio), so they must eat their own body weight in food every single day in order to stay alive. If they go without food for more than two hours, they can die. This means pygmy shrews are active both at night and during the day, all year round.

Maria Archbold

They eat many different things, including woodlice, beetles, flies, spiders, bugs, and insect larvae. Pygmy shrews living in Ireland eat lots of beetles, flies, and they especially love woodlice. Like rabbits and hares, pygmy shrews eat some of their own droppings in order to obtain the maximum energy from their food. This means they pass food through their stomach twice so that they can absorb all the nutrients and avoid waste. This is called 'refection'.

Breeding

Pygmy shrews mainly breed in June and July. The male and female do not stay together after mating and the female rears the young. The female is pregnant for about three weeks and gives birth to a litter of four to seven babies. Each newborn weighs only 0.25g, but they grow very quickly and leave their mother after just three weeks, when they are ready to fend for themselves. A female may give birth to a few litters each summer and the young females may themselves have families within just a few weeks.

Pygmy shrews don't live very long. Many die at just a few months old, and they probably only live about a year in the wild. But pygmy shrews have been around a long time. They have lived in Europe for at least two million years (modern humans, like you, have only been on the Earth for about 100 thousand years).

Irish bats

Leisler's bat

Brown long-eared bat

Natterer's bat

Daubenton's bat

Whiskered bat

Lesser horseshoe bat

Pipistrelles

Brown long-eared bat

Ialtóg fhad-chluasach
Plecotus auritus

Head and body length: 37-52mm
Weight: 6-12g

It is easy to understand where this bat gets its name. It has impressive long ears. Its ears are almost as long as its body. The brown long-eared bat is common throughout Ireland.

Home
During the summer months, female brown long-eared bats choose holes in trees and buildings for their maternity roosts. During winter they hibernate in caves or underground in mines, or in buildings, where they crawl into the small spaces behind tiles.

Diet
Most bats use loud calls in echolocation to help them locate prey. The long-eared bat whispers its echolocation calls but sometimes doesn't need to use these calls because it can hear the sounds the insect makes with its large ears. It simply follows the sound to catch its prey. Brown long-eared bats usually hunt among trees within a kilometre of their roost, where they spend the day.

Breeding
Brown long-eared bats gather to form maternity colonies in April each year. Both males and females are found together in these colonies. In June, a single bat is born to each mother.

Common pipistrelle
Ialtóg fheascrach
Pipistrellus pipistrellus
Head and body length: 40mm.
Weight: 4-8g

Soprano pipistrelle
Ialtóg fheascrach sopránach
Pipistrellus pygmaeus
Head and body length: 40mm
Weight: 4-8g

Nathusius' pipistrelle
Ialtóg Nathusius
Pipistrellus nathusii
Head and body: 46-55mm
Weight: 6-15g

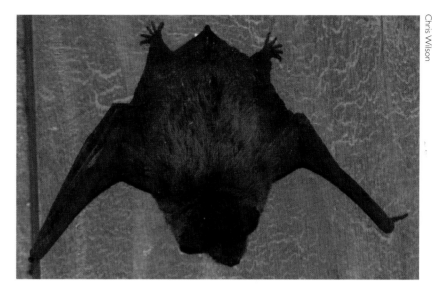

Chris Wilson

Bats cling onto a surface with their hind feet. They hang downwards, ready to take off in flight.

Pipistrelle Bats

There are three pipistrelle bats in Ireland – the common pipistrelle, the soprano pipistrelle and Nathusius' pipistrelle. These are the smallest of our bats and are closely related. The common pipistrelle is the most common bat seen in Ireland. The soprano and the common pipistrelle are found throughout the country. Nathusius' pipistrelle has been found at a number of places in the east of the country. Nathusius' pipistrelle has only been recorded in Ireland since 1996 so not much is known about its habits yet. Nathusius' pipistrelle is the biggest of the three.

Common and soprano pipistrelles usually make maternity roosts in buildings. They crawl into small spaces behind boards in the eaves of houses and behind tiles. Over winter, pipistrelles choose cool, dry sites, forming small groups in wall cavities, roofs or hollow trees for hibernation. Males and females roost together during hibernation, from November until late March.

Diet
Just before sunset, pipistrelles fly out from their roosts to look for insects. Common pipistrelles and Nathusius' pipistrelles forage in woodlands, over pasture, rivers and lakes. Soprano pipistrelles usually feed in areas close to water. They fly along the course of a river or stream and may travel three kilometres from their roost on a single night while searching for food. They may be small, but they are strong flyers! They can often be seen flying low over the surface of the water picking up gnats, tiny moths and caddis flies. Pipistrelles eat a wide variety of insects, including flies and midges.

Breeding
Pipistrelles mate in autumn. The male finds a breeding territory on a suitable tree, often near a hole. It flies back and forth from this breeding roost and uses a special call, the 'song-flight call' to attract females. Different species make different song-flight calls. One male may attract a number of females to its mating roost to breed. The following May, the females gather to form 'maternity roosts'. There are often over 100 bats in these colonies. They find sites that have just the correct temperature and conditions to keep their baby safe and warm. Males live in separate colonies during this time.

Between early June and July, the female gives birth to a single baby. On rare occasions twins are born. For the first week of life, the baby bat has no hair – this is why it is important that the maternity roost is warm and dry. The young baby is suckled on its mother's milk and grows very quickly. By mid-August, it no longer relies on its mother's milk and starts to fly. The mothers and young bats usually leave the maternity roosts by the end of August. Younger bats have darker fur than adults.

Leisler's bat has long dark golden
fur and a mousy face

Leisler's Bat

Ialtóg Leisler
Nyctalus leisleri

Head and body length: 50-70mm
Weight 12-20g

Leisler's bat is common and widespread throughout Ireland. It is quite rare in the rest of Europe and the Irish population is the biggest in Europe. This makes it very important that we protect this species.

Home
Leisler's bat usually roosts in buildings, behind fascia boards, in attics and under roof tiles, and in holes in trees. In winter, they use holes in trees and cracks in walls. Leisler's bats will sometimes travel up to 50 kilometres to find just the right hibernation site, where they will stay until spring.

Diet
Early in the evening, Leisler's bats leave their roosts and often travel over 10 kilometres from home to feed. Leisler's bats hunt over open fields and water. They feed on insects, such as midges, moths, caddis flies and crane flies. Because they begin to feed early in the evening, Leisler's bats also catch day-flying insects such as dung-flies.

Breeding
Some time between late summer and early autumn, the male Leisler's bat establishes a 'mating roost' on a tree and flies around the area calling for females. A single male can mate with a number of females. The following summer, the pregnant female joins a maternity colony and gives birth to a single baby in June. There can be up to 100 bats in the maternity colony.

The whiskered bat has a very dark face and wings.

Whiskered Bat

Ialtóg ghiobach
Myotis mystacinus

Head and body length: 35-48mm
Weight: 4-8g

The whiskered bat is a small bat. Its wings, face and ears are almost black. It has dark shaggy fur and its underbelly is grey. The Irish name, 'ialtóg ghiobach' means the 'shaggy bat' because of its appearance. The whiskered bat is found throughout Ireland.

Home

During the summer, whiskered bats usually roost in buildings and sometimes in trees. They climb into small spaces under tiles, roof slates and in stone walls.

Over winter they hibernate in mines, caves, and tunnels. Whiskered bats often share roosts with other bat species, so they may be more common than we think, but can be overlooked when roosting with other bats.

Diet

Whiskered bats feed in a range of habitats, including farmland, woodlands, in gardens and over water. They catch insects in flight so they are very agile flyers. They also pick insects off vegetation or from the ground. Prey includes small flies, spiders and moths.

Breeding

Mating usually occurs in autumn and sometimes during winter. Between May and August, females come together to form maternity colonies. The female whiskered bat gives birth to a single baby in June or early July.

Natterer's Bat

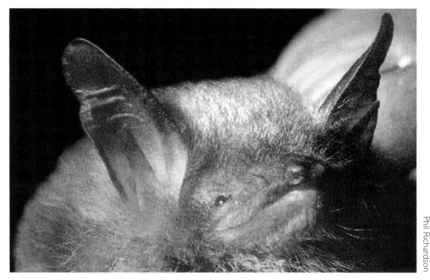

Phil Richardson

Natterer's bat has a pink face. Its upper body is brown, its belly white.

Ialtóg Natterer
Myotis nattereri

Head and body length: 45mm
Weight: 5-12g

Natterer's bat is found throughout Ireland where there is suitable woodland in order for it to find food. Natterer's bat has a pink face and white fur on its chest and belly. During the summer, Natterer's bats roost in trees and in old buildings and sometimes under old stone bridges. During the coldest period of winter, Natterer's bats use cold hibernation sites underground in caves, cellars, mines and tunnels. As temperatures rise again, Natterer's bats leave these hibernation roosts for roosts in trees and unoccupied buildings.

Diet
Natterer's bat only emerges after dark, late in the evening. It uses its tail membrane to help catch its prey. The tail membrane is a thin layer of skin between the bat's legs and tail. It uses it to scoop up insects, which it can then pass to its mouth.

Natterer's bats are excellent flyers and are very agile, flying easily between foliage and trees. They can catch insects in flight and also pick insects, spiders and caterpillars off vegetation. Like other bat species, Natterer's bats will carry a large insect, such as a moth or a beetle, back to a night roost before eating it.

Breeding
Mating usually occurs in autumn. The male establishes a mating roost on a suitable tree and calls to attract females. Mating can continue during the winter months. The following May, the females gather in maternity colonies where they will stay until September. In late June or early July, the female gives birth to a single baby.

Lesser horseshoe bat

Ialtóg crúshrónach / Crú-ialtóg beag
Rhinolophus hipposideros

Head and body length: 35-39mm
Wingspan: 25cm
Weight: 4-9g

The lesser horseshoe bat got its name because of the folds on its nose that make the shape of a horseshoe. This is called the face 'leaf' and helps the bat to detect the sounds used in echolocation. It is a tiny bat that hangs upside-down, with its wings wrapped around its body. Its ears do not have the 'tragus', the lobe found in the ears of other bats to help in echolocation.

Habitat & Home
The lesser horseshoe bat is found in suitable parts of the west of Ireland, between Mayo and Cork. In summer, lesser horseshoe bats need old unused stone buildings with slate roofs for their summer roosts. They use old uninhabited cottages, churches and outbuildings, which have large entrances to roof spaces, cellars, and attics. They like to be able to fly directly to their roosting areas, without interruption, so they choose buildings that have large entrances. This means that modern buildings are often unsuitable as they are built differently to the horseshoe's traditional buildings.

In winter, most lesser horseshoes hibernate in mines, caves, cellars or ice houses. They do not huddle in groups during hibernation. Though there may be a number of bats in a hibernation site, they do not hang close together.

Diet
At dusk, lesser horseshoes leave their roosts and fly low along the edges of buildings and hedgerows to areas of deciduous woodland. They will usually travel up to about two kilometres from their roosts to feed. They hunt for midges, moths, crane flies and caddis flies. They catch their prey in flight or pick them off vegetation.

Breeding
Mating occurs between September and April. Females gather in maternity colonies in late April and early May and each breeding female gives birth to a single baby in late June or early July. If the mother feels the maternity colony is in danger or the roost has been disturbed, she may carry her baby to a new roost. The young bat grows quickly and is independent after about five weeks.

RTE/Pat Falvey

The lesser horseshoe bat has a special horseshoe-shaped fold on its face that helps in echolocation. It emits sound through its nostrils instead of its mouth like most bats. This flap of skin directs its ultrasonic sounds to help the bat navigate and find its prey.

Conor Kelleher

The lesser horseshoe bat hangs upside-down with its wings wrapped around its body.

Daubenton's bats huddle together
for warmth in their roosts

Daubenton's bat

Ialtóg uisce
Myotis daubentonii

Head and body length: 50mm
Weight: 7-14g

Daubenton's bat is also known as the 'water bat' as it feeds by flying low across water and skimming insects from the surface and from the air above. It is found throughout Ireland. Its upper body is covered in brown fur and its underside is pale in colour.

During the summer months, Daubenton's bat roosts close to water in warm sites in holes in trees, in tunnels, in holes in the brickwork of bridges and in buildings near water. For winter, Daubenton's bat moves to roosts in underground sites in mines, caves and ice houses. It usually crawls into small cavities to hibernate.

Diet
Daubenton's bat emerges from its roost later in the evening than other bats. It is a fast, agile bat. It flaps its wings very quickly as it hunts over slow-moving water. It also forages among trees near water. It travels up to 10 kilometres from its roost to feed. It feeds on midges and other small flies, caddis flies, moths and mayflies.

Specialised for feeding over water, Daubenton's bat eats a lot of insects that emerge from water as they grow from their aquatic larval stage.

Breeding
During autumn, male and female Daubenton's bats come together to mate. The babies are born at the end of June. When they are about seven weeks old, they are weaned and can hunt for themselves.

This photograph of Daubenton's bat
shows the tiny size of our bats
against a brick wall.

Rabbit

Coinín
Oryctolagus cuniculus

Body length: 43cm
Tail: 7cm
Weight: 1.4-2kg

We don't know if there were rabbits in Ireland before the ice ages, but they have been introduced since then. In the 12th century, the Normans brought rabbits to Ireland as a source of meat and fur. We do know that rabbits were kept in warrens on Lambay Island in 1191; in Connacht in 1204; and in Ballysax, Co. Kildare, in 1282. They were kept in protected areas and given extra food, but many escaped and the Descendants of these rabbits adapted to life in Ireland's wild countryside very well. The rabbit is now an important prey species for foxes, stoats, badgers and birds of prey. Rabbits were originally only found on cliff tops, sand dunes and other areas of short grassland, but when humans started to clear forests and grow crops, farmland became ideal habitat for rabbits and they spread and increased in numbers.

The wild rabbit is grey-brown, fawn or sometimes even black in colour. Its underbelly is paler. Its white puffball tail, which is called a 'scut', is about 7cm long and has a black top. Rabbits have long hind legs. They keep their coats clean by grooming regularly. The rabbit is smaller than a hare and it has shorter ears and legs. Males are a little heavier than females. The male is called a 'buck', the female a 'doe', and the young are called 'kittens'.

Habitat & Home
Rabbits excavate a large burrow system called a 'warren'. Warrens are usually found at field edges, under hedgerows, brambles or scrub; where there is suitable grazing nearby, such as gardens, parks, golf courses, grassy cliff tops or farmland.

Diet
Rabbits eat many kinds of green plants and sometimes strip bark from trees. They usually leave their burrows after dark to feed. During the day, in order to get the most value out of the food they ate the night before, rabbits eat their droppings while resting in their burrows. This is called 'refection' and allows the rabbit to take in all the nutrients and vitamins from their food. Later, after dark, they will leave different droppings above ground. These are harder and darker and all of the nutrients and proteins have been removed.

Young rabbits are called 'kittens'. Kittens are furless and blind at birth. Fur the mother plucks from her chest is used to line the nest stop and keep the kittens warm. The mother may return only once each night for about five minutes to feed her young.

The entrance to a rabbit burrow. A warren has many entrances for a quick escape from predators.

Rabbits are very sociable animals and live in pairs or often in large groups. They establish a social order that includes dominant males and females. Dominant rabbits claim territory in the best part of the warren and are very successful at raising young. Rabbits usually stay close to their warren.

Rabbits are most active at night, but during the spring and summer months they are often seen above ground at dawn and dusk. In places where there is little hunting, rabbits may spend a lot of time above ground during daylight hours. You can spot a warren by the burrows and the very short grass in the area. You will also see the small round droppings that are often used to mark territories.

You find scrapes in the ground around a warren; these are also made to mark territories. They have a number of scent glands, including one under the chin, which they rub along the ground to tell other rabbits: "this place is occupied".

When a rabbit senses danger, it warns the other members of its family and the rest of the colony by thumping its hind foot on the ground. When other rabbits hear the noise, they run for the safety of their burrows.

Breeding

Rabbits are very successful breeders. A young female can have its own young when it's only four months old. Breeding can happen at any time, but mainly takes place between January and August. Males compete for access to females and will fight by kicking or boxing with their front legs. Young are born in a special breeding nest that the mother makes in a burrow with a dead-end, which is called a 'stop'. The mother lines the nesting stop with fur plucked from her chest.

About a month after mating, three to seven kittens are born in the nest-stop. The female never travels far from her kittens, but usually only returns once each night to feed her young for just a few minutes. When she leaves the burrow she covers the entrance well with vegetation to hide its location from predators. Kittens are born with their eyes closed and furless, but they grow quickly and their eyes open after about a week. When they are three weeks old, the kittens leave the nest to come above ground and after another week they can nibble on plants and no longer need their mother's milk.

In one year, a female rabbit could give birth to 20 babies. So why aren't we overrun by rabbits? Many rabbits die as a result of disease, bad weather, food shortages and predators. Only about one-quarter of rabbits live for more than a year.

Rabbits have very good senses of smell, sight, and hearing. A rabbit's eyes are very large and are located on the sides of their head so that they can see behind as well as in front of them, giving them almost 360° vision. This helps them to spot predators.

John Carey

Irish mountain hare

Giorria
Lepus timidus hibernicus

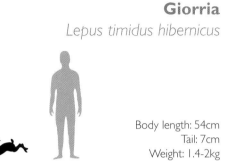

Body length: 54cm
Tail: 7cm
Weight: 1.4-2kg

The Mountain or Irish hare is one of Ireland's oldest mammals. The bones of an animal found in Co. Waterford are over 28,000 years old. The Irish mountain hare is different to mountain hares found in Britain and the rest of Europe. It does not turn white in winter so is known as a 'subspecies', meaning it is different to other populations. Male hares are called 'jacks', while females are called 'jills'. Young hares are called 'leverets'.

The mountain hare is much bigger than the rabbit and the female mountain hare is a little heavier than the male. The hind feet are very long. The mountain hare has long ears, slightly shorter than the length of its head, but the brown hare's ears are even longer, about the same length as its head. The coat of the Irish mountain hare is usually reddish brown in summer but changes to grey-brown in the winter months. Unlike brown hares, the top of the tail of the mountain hare is usually pale. Like rabbits, the hare's field of vision is almost 360° as the eyes are set in the sides of the head. This helps them to spot predators.

Habitat & Home

The Irish hare is found in every county in Ireland but numbers have decreased in recent years. It is found in open areas on uplands, farmland and grassland.

Mountain hares are usually nocturnal but are sometimes active during daylight in spring and summer. During the day, hares usually rest above ground in shallow depressions called 'forms', and in some areas will dig shallow burrows. At night they travel to foraging areas, sometimes covering large distances. Hares don't live in large groups like rabbits, but if there is enough food around they are usually happy to share the same area with other hares.

Diet

Irish hares eat many different plants, including heather, herbs, gorse, plantain, dandelions and grasses. Like rabbits, hares pass food through their bodies twice (known as 'refection') so that they can get the most nutrients from their food.

img_1

A hare stretches its legs.
The Irish mountain hare
can move very fast,
reaching speeds of up
to 60 miles per hour.

Richard T. Mills

Breeding

Breeding can take place throughout the year but mainly happens between January and September. There are often squabbles between males and females at this time and males fight over females. Males kick and box with their fore-legs and can be seen chasing each other, hence the phrase, "as mad as a March hare".

Breeding females usually have two or three litters each year. Pregnancy lasts about seven weeks and there are one to four leverets in each litter. The leverets are born with a full coat of fur and have their eyes open. During their first few days, the mother usually only visits them once each evening to feed them. A few days later, the leverets separate and spend their days alone, each in its own form. They come together again at feeding time to meet their mother. The leverets grow quickly and no longer need their mother's milk at just three weeks of age. Only about one-fifth of young hares survive their first year.

During the day, hares rest in 'forms', shallow depressions in the ground. Young hares are called 'leverets'.

Brown hare

Giorria gallda
Lepus europaeus

Body length: 55cm
Tail length: 10cm

The brown hare was first brought to Ireland by man in the late 1800s. Brown hares were released in parts of Cork, Armagh, Tyrone, Donegal, Wicklow, and Down. Today, it is found in parts of Northern Ireland but not in the Republic.

In Britain, where both the mountain hare and the brown hare are found, the mountain hare is usually found on upland areas, while the brown hare is common in fields and lowlands across the country. In Ireland it is a very different story. The mountain hare is found in farmland habitats, on lowlands as well as uplands across the country.

The brown hare's coat is usually yellowish brown in summer and more reddish brown in winter. The belly is white. It is not easy to distinguish between the mountain hare and the brown hare, but one clue is that the brown hare has a dark top on its tail, while the mountain hare's tail is pale or completely white. The brown hare is a little larger than the mountain hare. It also has longer ears and a darker coat than the mountain hare.

Brown hares are mainly nocturnal but like the Irish mountain hare, may be seen at dawn or dusk during spring and summer. They rest during the day in 'forms' in hedges or dense vegetation, and sometimes make shallow burrows. If you have ever seen a hare crouched in the middle of a field in the pouring rain, you will realise what hardy little animals these are. Imagine spending the winter months huddled on open ground all day long.

Diet
Brown hares usually eat grasses, herbs, cereal and root crops. In winter they sometimes strip bark from trees.

Breeding
Like mountain hares, brown hares are solitary animals but often feed alongside other hares and will form larger groups during the breeding season. Breeding occurs between February and October. Brown hares are seen 'boxing' and chasing each other during the courting season. Many leverets are killed by foxes, stoats and birds of prey. Others die as a result of cold, wet or disease.

Eddie Dunne

The brown hare has a more
mottled coat colour than the Irish
hare and a black top on its tail. The
brown hare's ears are about the
same length as its head.

Eddie Dunne

Eurasian Otter

Dobharchú / Madra uisce
Lutra lutra

Body length: Males 90cm; females 80cm
Tail length: 30-40cm
Weight: Males 11kg; females 7kg

The Eurasian otter has become extinct in much of Europe so Ireland's otter population is very important. In other countries, the otter has been persecuted through hunting and much of its natural habitat has been destroyed. The otter is one of our oldest mammals, having been found here since the end of the last ice age, about 10,500 years ago.

The otter's thick coat of fur is usually dark brown on its back and grey-brown on its belly. Unlike seals and cetaceans, otters do not have a thick layer of blubber to keep them warm. Instead, they have a very thick layer of fur next to the skin. This dense 'underfur' traps air and keeps the skin dry. The otter has small eyes and ears. Its body is long and streamlined for swimming. The otter usually dives under water for less than a minute at a time, but it has large lungs that help it to stay under water for several minutes. During dives, its heart rate also slows down so it can conserve oxygen. Its long stiff whiskers are important sense organs for finding food after dark or in murky water. Its feet are webbed, making it an excellent swimmer. These special adaptations equip the otter for life in water. Females are a much smaller than males.

Habitat & Home

Otters are found in rivers, lakes, marshes, estuaries and around the coast. Coastal otters must visit freshwater streams and rivers often in order to wash salt from their fur. Otters prefer areas of thick vegetation in which to make their homes. The otter digs a burrow in the riverbank, called a 'holt', where it rests during the day. It may use a number of holts under the edge of a riverbank or among the root systems of trees. Holts often have a number of entrances, some of which open under water. Otters will also sometimes use vacant rabbit burrows or fox earths if they are near water. Otters are territorial and usually live alone. A male ('dog') may use the same stretch of water as a female ('bitch') but it will not tolerate another male in its territory.

Otters are quiet, shy animals that are mainly active at dusk or after dark, so they are not often seen by humans. However, they do leave evidence of their whereabouts. They wear away pathways where they enter the water and you may find fish remains in the area.

The otter has a layer of dense underfur that traps air and insulates the skin. The longer outer fur forms a waterproof barrier, protecting the underfur and keeping the skin dry. The otter's feet are webbed to help it swim.

Billy Clarke

Otters are very playful animals. Even adult otters seem to enjoy sliding around on muddy banks. They will use the same slippery chutes to propel themselves into the water, and climb out just to enjoy the ride once again – just like a child on a playground slide. Solitary otters are also seen playing catch with pebbles – taking them in their mouths, throwing them in the air and catching them again.

Otters mark their territories with their black droppings, called 'spraints', often at noticeable points such as rocks or high mounds. These favourite spots are called 'seats' and are usually found at important fishing or grooming sites.

Diet

Otters are carnivores and usually catch fish that swim along the bottom of rivers and lakes. They sometimes eat water birds, small mammals and dead animals they might come across. Coastal otters eat crabs, molluscs, sea urchins and small fish. Otters usually hold their prey with their front paws while eating.

Breeding

Males and females come together to breed in spring and summer. Pregnancy lasts for about nine weeks and the female chooses a quiet area in her territory to make her breeding holt. Cubs are covered with fur when born but their eyes remain closed until they are about five weeks old. There are usually two or three cubs in each litter and they are fed by their mother until they are about four months old. The cubs will stay with their mother for between six months and a year; then they disperse to find their own territories. They usually begin to breed in their third year and otters probably only survive to five years of age in the wild.

Badger

Broc
Meles meles

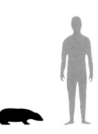

Body Length: male 75cm; female 70cm
Tail length: 15 cm
Weight: male 10-17kg; female 9-12kg

The badger is a beautiful animal with black and white stripes on its face. It is a stout animal with a grey coat and dark underside and legs. It has short, strong legs and a short bushy tail. Its ears are small, but it has good hearing. The badger has five very strong claws on each foot, which help it to dig. It also has very powerful jaws so it has a very strong bite. It does not have good eyesight but can see much better at night than humans can, since it is a nocturnal animal. It also has a very good sense of smell, which helps it to find food. If a badger is frightened, it can run quite quickly and can also swim well. The female is a little smaller than the male.

Family

The male badger is called a 'boar' and the female is called a 'sow'. Young are called 'cubs'. Badgers live in family groups. They dig a large underground home called a 'sett', which is made up of many tunnels and chambers. Each generation of badgers add new tunnels and entrances to the sett so that it keeps getting larger. Other mammals, such as foxes and otters, will move into disused badger setts. A fox will even sometimes move in when badgers still live there. The badger has special scent glands which it uses to mark its territory and other members of its social group.

Habitat & Home

Badgers usually make their homes in woodland areas, but they are also seen on farmland, uplands and in gardens. Over half of Irish badger setts are found under hedgerows.

Each territory controlled by a family of badgers contains one main sett and a few smaller setts. The main sett usually has about six entrances. A badger territory in Ireland can have between two and 20 badgers living together, but there are usually four or five animals in each main sett.

Badgers spend a lot of time digging tunnels and extending their setts. They sleep in special nest chambers, which they line with dried grass, straw and leaves. They are very fussy about their homes. They carry old nesting material back above ground to air it or dump it. They also leave the sett to use outdoor toilet areas or

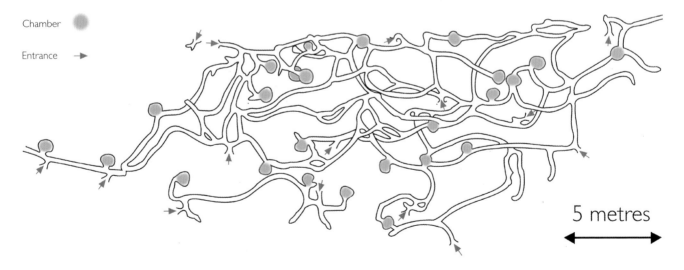

Chamber

Entrance →

5 metres

This is a map of a badger sett that was excavated by zoologists from University College Dublin. Zoologists are scientists who study animals. They found 25 sleeping chambers in this sett. There were 14 entrances and the tunnels ran for almost 300 metres. There were only five badgers living in this mansion!

'latrines' away from the sett. Latrines are used to mark the boundaries of their territory.

Over winter, badgers may become less active and their temperature can drop, allowing them to use less energy. This is a slight form of torpidity, but does not mean they hibernate. They build up fat reserves before winter and are heaviest in November and December.

Breeding

In Ireland, four or five badgers usually live together in a territory. There is usually one dominant male in each territory and usually only one female rears a litter each year. Mating usually occurs between April and May. After a delay, gestation usually begins in late December and lasts for about eight weeks. Cubs are born in a special 'birth chamber' in the sett in February or March. There are usually two or three badgers per litter. They are blind when they are born and their eyes do not open until they are about five weeks old, so they rely completely on their mother. They begin to explore the world above ground at about seven weeks of age and are weaned after three to five months.

Here is a busy badger leaving its sett. 'Brochach' is the Irish name for a badger sett

Richard Mills

Diet

Badgers eat both plants and animals so we call them 'omnivores'. Badgers eat beetles, snails, slugs, cockchafers, frogs, frogspawn, small mammals, cereals, blackberries, apples, acorns, mushrooms, clover and grass. Badgers especially love eating earthworms, their most common food. A badger can eat up to 200 earthworms in one night.

Badger facts

When scientists first described the badger in the 18th century, they thought it was a small bear. Do you think it looks a bit like a bear? Badger setts are among the biggest structures ever made by an animal other than man. One sett found in Dublin, that was studied by zoologists from University College Dublin was found to have 25 chambers and 260 metres of tunnels. Badgers are always busy, digging more tunnels and improving their homes.

The badger lives on a diet almost entirely made up of plant roots and earthworms

Badgers are very clean animals. They regularly change their bedding. They carry out old nesting material by balancing it between their chin and forelegs. When carrying in new nesting material, they carefully move backwards into the tunnel entrance.

78

Red Fox

Sionnach / Madra Rua
Vulpes vulpes

Body length: 55-60 cm
Tail length 40cm
Weight: male 6-7kg; female 5-6kg

The fox is common throughout Ireland. It is a beautiful, clever animal. Like our domesticated pet dogs, the fox shares ancestors with the wolf. The fox has a beautiful reddish-brown coat of fur and a long bushy tail called a 'brush', which has a white tip. Sometimes, greyish or almost black foxes are seen. When it is fully grown, the fur on its feet and legs is black so an adult fox looks like it's wearing black socks. The fox has a long narrow white muzzle or snout, and black-tipped ears. As winter approaches, the coat becomes thicker to protect the animal in cold weather.

A fully-grown fox is about the same size as a large domestic cat. Males are a little larger than females. The female fox is called a 'vixen'; the male a 'dog'; and young are called 'cubs'.

Habitat & Home

The fox can live in many different habitats. It is found in woodland, on farmland, bogs, mountains, coastal areas, and they have even moved into our towns and cities. Foxes have adapted well to living near man, in suburbs and town parks. They have learned to make homes in old buildings, drains and under sheds. Because they are nocturnal, which means they are most active at night, they can look for food when most of us are asleep. They are very clever animals and have learned to 'scavenge' as well as hunt – this means they can find food in our dumps, dustbins and litter. Urban foxes will also finish off any pet food left out in gardens overnight for our well-fed dogs and cats. They are very agile and can move through towns by jumping up onto high walls and climbing trees.

The fox digs an underground home called an 'earth' where it can stay in bad weather. They usually make their earths under hedgerows, in rock crevices, drains or buildings. Sometimes a fox will live in an old rabbit burrow or badger sett. The vixen gives birth to her cubs in the earth. In good weather, foxes like to lie above ground but are very careful to keep hidden in case of danger.

Life isn't always easy for our wild animals. They must survive through our coldest winters. And they constantly have to find food for themselves and for their young – no matter what the weather.

Habits

The dog has a high-pitched bark and vixens make ear-piercing screams. In the past, people used to think the sound of a vixen's scream was the wail of a banshee. The fox's eyesight is best in low light, which means it can see much better after dark than humans can. It has a very good sense of smell and uses special scent glands to mark its territory and communicate with other foxes. Like other mammals, they can smell markings left by other foxes and this tells them whether they are male or female and whether the female is ready to breed.

The fox has excellent hearing, which helps it to hunt its prey. Its hearing is so good in fact, it can even hear earthworms, insects and mice as they move along the ground. Foxes usually live in pairs – one male and one female that produce young. Where conditions are good, they may also live in larger family groups – usually containing one adult male and one breeding female, along with other non-breeding females, which help to take care of and play with the cubs.

Diet

The fox is opportunistic, and is flexible in what it eats and where it lives. It eats rabbits, young hares, mice, rats, birds and their eggs, and dead animals. A fox will also eat beetles and other insects, earthworms, mushrooms, and fruits such as blackberries and apples. If they live by the sea, foxes will eat fish and crabs that they find on the shore.

Fox cubs spend a lot of time playing and exploring their surroundings. They are curious animals. The fox moves more like a cat than a dog. It is very agile, can jump and climb well and pounces on its prey.

Foxes have become quite common in our towns and cities. A fox may visit your garden and become quite used to humans.

Philip Smyth

Mike Brown

Breeding

Breeding takes place over winter, between December and early February. Young males and females often bark and use scent to find each other. A dog and vixen often stay together for a number of years. Males sometimes fight for access to a female, but they usually don't bite each other as this would cause too much damage. Instead, they check the other animal's strength by noticing its size, shape, teeth, or by wrestling.

Gestation lasts for almost two months and cubs are born between February and April. A vixen has one litter per year, usually of four or five cubs. For the first few weeks, the vixen stays in its earth with the cubs, which are blind and deaf when born, and the dog fox brings her food. Later, the vixen may be seen above ground during the day as she looks for food. The cubs have darker fur and blue eyes at birth. If the female has to move the cubs to another earth, she carries them, one by one in her mouth, carefully holding them by the scruff of the neck. At four weeks their eyes change colour to the amber of the adult, and the red coat begins to grow. When the cubs are seven months old, they are almost fully grown and males and many females leave their mothers around November to find their own territories. Many foxes don't survive their first year, and the most successful animals won't usually live longer than four years in the wild.

Pine marten

Cat crainn
Martes Martes

Body and tail length: male 66-73cm;
female 61-66cm
Weight: male 1.5-1.9kg; female 1.1-1.5kg

The Irish name for the pine marten means 'tree-cat'. This beautiful animal is very agile and a great climber, like a cat, and it spends much of its time in the treetops. It is an animal of coniferous forests, but has adapted to other habitats in Ireland. Strong populations are found in the Burren, in Killarney National Park, the Slieve Bloom Mountains, and in parts of Meath and Waterford. It used to be much more common throughout Ireland, but hunting led to its decline. Today, it is again beginning to spread into other parts of the country, including Kildare, Laois, Wicklow, Dublin, Carlow, Fermanagh, Antrim, Tyrone and Down.

The pine marten has a long snout, with a yellow patch running from its chin to its chest. Otherwise its coat is dark, chocolate brown, and it has a reddish belly. It has large rounded ears and long whiskers. Its tail is long and bushy. The pine marten has large feet with long sharp claws that help it to climb. It can jump from branch to branch and it stretches out its long tail to help its balance. The pine marten has excellent senses of smell, hearing and eyesight.

Habitat

The pine marten is found mainly in coniferous or deciduous woodlands, and areas of scrub. It has also adapted to pasture, moors and coastal areas. It survives well among the hazel scrub and limestone pavements of the Burren in Co. Clare.

Habits

The pine marten is 'solitary', meaning it lives alone. Males and females are territorial, defending separate territories. They have scent glands that they use, along with their droppings and urine, to mark their territories. They mark pathways, rocks and important points around their homes. It is nocturnal, being active at night. During the summer, females may be seen during daylight hours when they are hunting for extra food for their young. The pine marten is usually quite shy and wary of humans, but if food is left out regularly, or if it makes a den in a building, it can become quite used to humans.

The pine marten uses nest sites or 'dens' made in hollows in trees, crevices in rocks, or large old birds' nests or squirrel dreys. They line the nest with dried grass. They may also make homes in old buildings. The pine marten often has a number of dens in its territory and may travel 20 kilometres in one night as it searches for food.

Diet

The pine marten eats small birds and small mammals, berries, mushrooms, and invertebrates, and dead animals it finds ('carrion'). It usually hunts on the ground, and will eat earthworms, beetles, rats, wood mice, leverets, rabbits, frogs and nestlings. On the coast it also eats fish and crabs.

Breeding

Breeding take place once a year, between August and September. After a period of delayed pregnancy, gestation lasts about a month, and young are usually born between late March and April. Litters range from one to five kits.

Kits are deaf, blind and are covered in short grey fur at birth. When they are about seven weeks old, they start to leave the den for short periods. They are weaned a few weeks later, but stay with their mother until August or September, when they leave to find territories of their own. Pine martens can survive to five or six years of age in the wild.

The pine marten's coat is chocolate brown and its tail is long and bushy. It has large rounded ears and long whiskers.

Eddie Dunne

Irish stoat

Easóg
Mustela erminea hibernicus

Length (nose to tail tip): male 31-39cm;
female 24-29cm
Weight: males 200-400g; females 100-200g

The stoat in Ireland is very different to stoats found in other countries, so we call it a 'subspecies'. It has lived in Ireland for many thousands of years. The bones of a stoat found in a cave in Cork are 35,000 years old. Irish people often call the stoat a 'weasel', but the weasel is a different animal and it is not found in Ireland.

The male stoat is larger than the female. Stoats in the south of the country are larger than those in the north. It has a long slim body. Its fur coat is chestnut brown on top and the throat and belly are white. The division between the dark upper fur and the white patch is usually an irregular line, whereas this is a straight dividing line in stoats in other countries. The Irish stoat does not turn white in winter like stoats in Britain and much of Europe. Its tail has a black tip and it is not as fluffy or long as that of a pine marten. It has small ears and beady eyes. The stoat has a good sense of smell, hearing and very good eyesight. It has quite short legs, but can move very quickly and chase down much larger prey.

Habitat & Home
The stoat can adapt well in different habitats and is found in hedgerows, forest, moorland, marsh, scrub and in upland areas. It makes its den in hollow trees, clefts in rocks and in rabbit burrows. It will sometimes use old buildings.

The stoat is a very agile and fast animal. It is quite curious and playful. They use visual signals and scent to communicate with each other. The stoat is solitary and territorial. It may use a number of dens in its territory. They use special scent glands and their droppings to mark their territories and they use the same routes and paths each night as they hunt for food. During the spring and summer they are usually diurnal and may be seen during the day as they search for food. In autumn and winter they usually hunt after dark and rest in one of their dens during daylight.

A stoat can kill an animal that is five times its own weight. They hide food that they don't eat straight away.

The stoat can climb well and will hunt above and below ground in animal burrows. It often uses strange movements, standing on its hind legs and weaving its body – like a sort of dance – to confuse or 'hypnotise' its prey, before attacking and biting the back of the neck to kill it quickly. It is a determined hunter and will follow its prey for miles if necessary, in and out of underground burrows.

Diet

The stoat is a carnivore, or meat-eater, but it is flexible and will eat whatever is available, including rabbits, rats, mice, shrews, pigeons, songbirds, nestlings, insects and other invertebrates. It uses hiding places for food it doesn't finish straight away. A stoat can kill an animal up to five times its own weight. Because it is a small slim animal, it loses heat quickly so it must eat regularly. A stoat must consume 20% of its body weight in food every day.

Breeding

Stoats breed once each year, between May and July. After a delay, gestation lasts for about one month. Young stoats are called 'kits' and are usually born the following April or May. There are between three and 10 kits in each litter. Kits are deaf and blind at birth and are covered in greyish fur. At five weeks old, they start to eat solid food and soon begin to accompany their mother as she teaches them to hunt.

They are weaned by 12 weeks, when they are able to hunt for themselves and may leave their mother to find territories of their own. Many kits die over winter and survivors probably only live to four years of age.

The Irish stoat can be seen hunting among the dry-stone walls and limestone pavements of the Burren in Co Clare. Because they are very curious animals, it is sometimes possible to watch them and photograph them watching you.

American Mink

Minc Mheiriceánach
Mustela vison

Body length: 42-50cm
Tail length: 12cm
Weight: Males 0.9-1.3kg; females 0.5-0.8kg

Mink found in the wild in Ireland are descended from animals that escaped from fur farms. The animal began to breed in the wild in the 1950s, and is now found throughout the country. Mink bred in fur farms usually have pale-coloured coats, but in the wild the population begins to grow darker coats again and most wild mink are dark brown to black, with a white patch on the neck. They have long tails and their feet are partly webbed to help them swim. The mink spends most of its time close to water and is sometimes confused with the otter, but it is smaller, slimmer, and has a more pointed snout.

Habitat & Home
Mink are now found throughout the country, along rivers, streams, canals, lakes and along the coast. Mink live in dens made in old rabbit burrows, hollow trees or sometimes in old buildings. They usually choose areas where thick vegetation offers cover. Sometimes they will dig their own burrows in soft soil and will often use a number of different dens. Mink usually live alone and are territorial.

Diet
The mink is a carnivore and will eat any suitable prey, including slow-swimming fish, freshwater crayfish, rabbits, rats, insects, frogs and water birds. When hunting, it will dive on prey from the riverbank or from overhanging trees. Mink are most active after dark. Mink use their long whiskers to sense fish in murky water and their eyes are also adapted to seeing under water.

Breeding
Breeding takes place between February and April. Males often fight for access to females, by hissing, screaming, wrestling and biting. Gestation lasts for about one month. Young mink are called 'kits' and are furless, blind and deaf at birth. One litter of three to five kits are born in April or May. They are weaned after about two months when they can hunt with their mother. In August or September, the young are fully grown and leave home to find their own territories. Many young animals die if they cannot find their own suitable territory but may live to four years of age in the wild.

Mink have long slim
bodies and can squeeze
through tight spaces.

The mink's dark brown
coat can look black when
wet. The female mink is
smaller than the male.

Red Deer

Fia rua
Cervus elaphus

Height (to shoulder): stag: 120-140cm;
hind: 90-100cm
Weight: stag 200kg; hind 100-130kg

Adult male red deer are called 'stags', females 'hinds', and young deer are called 'calves'. The red deer is the largest of our wild deer. Populations are now found in counties Tyrone, Down, Fermanagh, Donegal, Wicklow, Kerry and Meath. The Wicklow red deer population have interbred with introduced sika deer to produce hybrids.

The coat of the red deer changes colour through the year. In winter, it can be grey to brown, and during the breeding season males grow a long shaggy mane around their necks. In summer, red deer look more reddish-brown in colour. They have a line along their backs, with small white spots on either side. The fur on the belly is grey.

Calves are reddish brown and they have much more obvious white spots on their sides. Like other deer, red deer have a 'rump patch' – a patch of lighter fur under their tail. If a deer is frightened, the sight of this rump patch as the animal runs away is a warning to other deer that they may be in danger. The red deer has a short tail that hangs halfway down the rump patch.

Only the stags grow antlers, which are replaced each year. The antlers tend to become larger and have more points (called 'tines') with each year. Red deer and their antlers vary greatly in size depending on the food they can find to eat and where they live. The antlers are shed in spring and a new set begin to grow. They are covered in a skin called 'velvet' as they grow and are fully grown by August. This is when the velvet dies and falls off to reveal the new clean antlers. When the young male calves are about seven months old, their antlers begin to grow.

Habitat & Home

Red deer in Ireland are usually found in secluded woodlands or upland moors and mountainous areas. They often use coniferous woodlands.

Red deer are active both during the day and at night, but feed mainly in the early hours of the morning and late in the evening. When not feeding, they spend time lying under cover and chewing the cud or ruminating. Males and females usually live in separate herds. Female groups usually consist of adult females, their daughters and their calves, and one-year old males. There are usually five to seven females in a group, while male groups are usually smaller.

A male red deer, a 'stag'. Stags shed their antlers once each year in spring and new ones begin to grow. They are fully grown by August.

A female red deer, a 'hind'. One aid to identifying red deer is by the length of the tail and its pale rump patch. The red deer's tail hangs halfway down its rump patch.

A red deer hind. Only the stags have antlers.

Diet

Red deer are opportunistic, which means they eat a variety of foods, depending on what is available. They eat leaves, grasses, herbs, woody shoots, fruits and acorns. They sometimes strip bark from trees.

Special stomachs

The deer and feral goat found in Ireland are herbivores, meaning they eat green vegetation. They have very complex digestive systems to allow them to obtain all of the energy and nutrients they require from plants. Mammals cannot digest cellulose, which is found in the cell walls of plants. But some animals, including deer, sheep and cattle, have evolved a special way of consuming cellulose. They have special micro-organisms living in a chamber in their stomachs, called the 'rumen' – these micro-organisms can break down cellulose into forms that the animal can digest. This relationship between the mammal and the micro-organisms that live in its gut is called 'symbiosis'. It means that both parties benefit from the arrangement – the micro-organisms are provided with plant food on which they can grow and multiply, while the mammal benefits by being able to absorb nutrients from cellulose, which would otherwise be indigestible.

Herbivores have special chambers in their stomachs where these micro-organisms live. It is here that they break down cellulose by a process called 'fermentation'. Deer and goats have four of these chambers in their stomachs. Because plant material is very tough they spend a lot of time chewing their food. They even bring food back from their stomachs to grind it up again with their teeth – this is called "chewing the cud". This is why you may see cattle or sheep lying down in a field having a good chew even though they don't seem to be taking in any grass. They are 'ruminating' or chewing the cud. This is why deer, cattle, sheep and goats are called 'ruminants'.

It is important not to disturb deer herds. When food is scarce, especially in spring, it is important that deer are left in peace to feed. Otherwise they can lose weight and condition.

Breeding

Breeding occurs between late September and November, a time called the 'rut'. From August onwards, stags begin to join the herds of hinds. During the rut males compete for access to females and will roar and fight with other males. They fight by locking antlers and wrestling each other back and forth with their antlers. They also develop a very strong smell at this time and will thrash at trees with their antlers to show their strength. Red deer have scent glands on their faces, which they use to mark their surroundings during the rut.

Males do not usually get to mate until they are five years old because they usually have to compete with older stronger males. A breeding stag tries to attract and defend a number of females, a 'harem'. This will allow it to father as many young as possible. Gestation lasts for about six months and usually a single calf is born between May and June. For the first few days of life, calves usually stay hidden by lying in thick vegetation. If you come across a deer calf on its own, this does not mean it has been abandoned by its mother; she is probably very close by. Touching or moving calves can lead to abandonment, as the smell of humans may lead to the mother rejecting it so it is best to leave the area as quickly as possible.

In its second week the calf begins to follow its mother. Calves are weaned by the time they are eight months old. When male calves are about one year old, they leave the herd of hinds and join a male group. Stags usually live to about 12 years of age, while hinds may survive for 20 years.

Billy Clarke

During the 'rut', stags roar to attract females (opposite page). They also like to 'wallow' or roll in mudpools. They want to increase their scent as much as possible so they are noticed by females.

For the first few days of life, red deer calves usually hide by lying in thick vegetation.

During the rut, stags compete for access to females. They lock horns and wrestle to test each other's strength.
Young stags practise for when it will be their turn to breed.

Philip Smyth

Vincent McGoldrick

A beautiful red stag. During the
breeding season, the stag grows a
long shaggy mane around its neck.

Opposite page: fallow deer range in colour
from white to black. The males are called
'bucks' and have beautiful antlers.

Fallow Deer

Fia buí
Dama dama

Height (to shoulder): males 100cm;
females 80-85cm
Weight: males 100kg; females 40-45kg

Fallow deer are our most widespread deer. They were first brought to Ireland by the Normans in the 13th century. Fallow deer are often kept in parks but escapees do very well in the wild. Today, fallow deer are found in every county in Ireland. Male fallow deer are called 'bucks', females 'does', and young are called 'fawns'.

The coat of the fallow deer varies from white to black. Most have a white rump patch surrounded by a heart-shaped black line. Black fallow deer and white fallow deer do not show this line. There is a dark stripe on the back, and most show white spots on their sides. In winter these white spots fade to grey and are less noticeable. In most, the belly is pale in colour. The fallow deer has a longer tail than the other Irish deer. It falls below the rump patch. The buck sheds its antlers between March and May and a new set is fully grown by August.

Habitat & Home
Fallow deer can be found in deciduous woodland with access to open grasslands. They eat mainly grass, but may also eat herbs, fruits and leaves.

Active both night and day, fallow deer usually graze in the early morning and just before dark. Fallow deer often form large herds. Males and females live in separate groups.

Mature bucks (males) have antlers with broad, flattened tips. The fallow deer has a longer tail than the red deer or sika deer, falling below the rump patch.

During the rut, bucks compete for access to does.

Breeding

The breeding season or 'rut' takes place in October. Bucks join the groups of does and become quite aggressive, letting out loud 'groans' to warn off other males. Bucks mark their surroundings with special oil produced by scent glands on the face. They also urinate on themselves so that they give off a very strong musky smell. Bucks will regularly fight for access to females. Bucks fight in the same way as other deer – by locking their antlers together and wrestling and pushing each other in either direction. This allows the buck to test its opponent's strength. The stronger animal wins access to the female herd and he will mate with as many does as he can to father many fawns.

Gestation in fallow deer lasts for over seven months. Usually a single fawn is born in June. In order to avoid predators such as foxes, the fawn stays resting in thick cover for its first two weeks of life. The mother returns to feed her young and then leaves it again to allow it to hide. After this vulnerable period, the fawn is more steady on its feet and follows its mother. The fawn is weaned before it is a year old.

During its first few days of life, a fawn hides in long grass during the day.

Richard Mills

Sika deer

Fia Seapánach
Cervus nippon

Height (to shoulder): Stag 75-80cm;
hind 65-70cm
Weight: stag 50-60kg; hind 30-35kg

Sika deer were introduced into Ireland from Japan in 1860 when Lord Powerscourt brought a small herd to his park at Powerscourt, Co Wicklow. Sika deer from this first herd were later released in parks in Kerry, Fermanagh, Limerick, Monaghan and Down. Sika deer did very well in the Irish countryside and many escaped from deer farms to establish wild populations. Today, sika deer are found in Donegal, Cavan, Tyrone, Fermanagh, Dublin, Kildare, Wicklow, Carlow, Wexford, Kilkenny, Cork and Kerry. In some areas, such as Wicklow, sika have interbred with red deer over the years to produce hybrids. Sika deer are also found in Killarney National Park alongside our native red deer, but do not seem to have interbred with the red deer there. Male sika deer are called 'stags', females 'hinds', and the young are known as 'calves'.

The sika deer is the smallest wild deer found in Ireland. The females are smaller than the males. The coat colour ranges from light to dark brown with light spots and a dark stripe along the back. The underside is light grey. In winter, the coat is darker, becoming grey to black in colour. Stags grow a shaggy mane around the breeding season or 'rut'. Sikas have a white rump patch surrounded by a line of dark hair. If a sika is scared and runs away, the sight of the white rump patch warns other deer of danger. The stags grow antlers, which are shed each year in spring and re-grow by August.

Habitat
Sika deer in Ireland are often found in conifer plantations and semi-natural woodland. In summer, when cover is good, sika deer move out into areas of thick bracken.

Diet
Sika deer normally feed in the early morning and late evening, but they may be active both day and night. Sika deer are opportunistic feeders, meaning they have a very varied diet and eat whatever of their foods are most available. They eat leaves, herbs, acorns, tree shoots, fruit, grasses, cereals and root crops.

Female sika deer are called 'hinds'. Calves are born in May or June and are fed on their mothers' milk for about seven months.

Habits

Sika hinds live together in groups of up to 10 animals. These groups are usually made up by adult hinds, their daughters, and young male and female calves. Sika stags usually live on their own, but join herds during the rut.

Breeding

The breeding season, the 'rut', occurs between late August and early December. You may hear the 'whistles' and moans of the stags during this time. Stags compete for access to hinds and will fight with each other by locking antlers and wrestling in a test of strength. The strongest stag wins access to the hinds so they will father the calves born the following year. During the rut, the sika stag uses an oil secreted by scent glands on its face to mark surrounding vegetation. They also thrash at trees with their antlers at this time.

Pregnancy last for about seven months and usually a single calf is born in May or June. The calf usually rests in a hiding place for its first few days. After two weeks it begins to follow its mother as she feeds. It is fed on its mother's milk until it is about seven months old.

John Carey

Feral Goat

Gabhar fiáin
Capra hircus

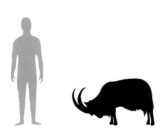

Weight: Males 50-75kg;
females 35-60kg

Wild or feral goats in Ireland descended from domestic animals that were kept by humans. They were probably brought to Ireland about 4,000 years ago. People kept goats for milk and skins. Goat's hair was used to make wool, paintbrushes, wigs and rope, while the skin was used to make liquid containers, early paper and bodhráns. Many of these domestic animals probably escaped and became wild, and their descendants are now found in remote mountainous areas, hilltops and on cliffs. Feral goat populations are regularly joined by goats that escape from farms and unwanted animals that are simply let loose. There are herds in the Burren, Co. Clare; Killarney, Co. Kerry; and Glendalough, Co. Wicklow.

We call male goats 'billies', females 'nannies', and the young we call 'kids'. The feral goats' thick coats may be white, grey, brown or black, in a variety of patterns. Both males and females have horns, but the male's horns are larger than the female's.

There are usually 12 or more female goats in a herd, usually led by an older dominant nanny. Males are usually seen in separate smaller groups. Dominant animals are often the oldest and strongest in a group, and dominant males may have impressive horns, up to about half a metre in length. Large herds of up to 100 animals are sometimes seen. In bad weather or while ruminating, goats rest in the shelter of scrub, woodland, caves or in rocky places.

Diet
Feral goats browse on shrubs, gorse and woody plants, and graze on herbs, sedges, rushes, bilberry and heather. Goats are famous for eating everything and anything, and for feral goats this includes seaweed around our coasts. They also eat shoots and leaves, strip bark and nibble young trees.

Breeding

Breeding occurs between August and December, and this time is called the 'rut'. Billies develop a strong musky smell during the rut as they have many scent glands, on their feet, behind their horns, and near their tail. Billies show off their strength to other males by shaking their heads, lowering their horns, and if necessary by fighting. They will butt heads in competition for females. They rear up on their hind legs to deliver the hardest blows.

Most nannies start to breed at a year old. Gestation lasts about 5 months, and most kids are born between February and April. Nannies usually give birth to one or two kids. In their first week of life, kids hide in vegetation or amongst rocks. After this, they follow their mothers until they are weaned at about six months. If they survive their first most difficult year, goats may live to about 8 years of age.

In winter, the goat's hair grows quite long and the male grows a mane along its neck. Both males and females have horns and all males and many females have long shaggy beards. The age of a goat can be estimated by counting the 'growth rings' on their horns.

Goats have a large spongy pad under each hoof. This helps them to keep their balance on steep slopes and high mountainside rocks.

John Carey

Grey seal

Rón mór
Halichoerus grypus

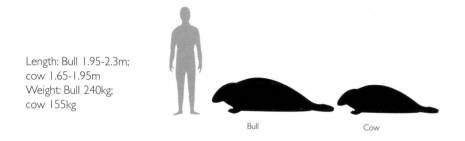

Length: Bull 1.95-2.3m;
cow 1.65-1.95m
Weight: Bull 240kg;
cow 155kg

Bull

Cow

The grey seal is the seal most frequently seen around Irish coasts. Grey seals make a lot of noises – moaning, hissing, rumbling and barking – so where they haul out can be noisy places. Grey seals are more aggressive than common seals. You may see common seals basking alongside grey seals. Besides basking in the sun and breeding on land, grey seals spend much of their time at sea. Male seals are called 'bulls', females 'cows', and young seals are called 'pups'.

When the grey seal's coat is wet, it looks almost black, but when dry, it is mottled grey or brownish-grey. Cows are paler and slimmer than bulls. The spots or blotches on the grey seal are larger than those on the common seal. The grey seal is also larger than the common seal and it has a flat head and parallel nostrils, while the common seal's nostrils form a V-shape. The bull has a long pointed face and a thick broad neck with many folds of skin, while the sow's muzzle is shorter, and she has a thinner neck. In March, grey seals moult their coats and will spend long periods lying on rocks until they are cloaked in their new bright coats.

Diet
Grey seals eat a variety of fish, including salmon, mackerel, herring, whiting, sandeels, flatfish, ling and cod. They are 'opportunistic', hunting whatever is available, and will eat seabirds, squid and crustaceans.

Grey seal pups are covered
in creamy-white fur at birth.
This is moulted after about
three weeks and is replaced
by a shorter coat.

The male grey seal, called a 'bull', is larger than the female. It has a long snout and is two metres or more in length when fully grown.

Breeding

In August and September, large numbers of grey seals gather on land. Pregnant grey seal cows come ashore to give birth; and bulls come ashore because the mating season is about to start. Cows usually return to the same breeding ground each year and even find the same spot where they gave birth the year before, which they defend from other females. Breeding colonies are usually found on sandbanks or rocky shores.

The cow gives birth to a single pup, which it will feed on its rich milk for about three weeks. Grey seal pups are covered in creamy-white fur when they are born. This is moulted after about three weeks and is replaced with a fawn-coloured coat. The young seal begins to swim after a few weeks and starts to hunt a few weeks

RTE/Don Wycherley

A female grey seal

after it is weaned. Many pups die in their first year, due to drowning in storms, starvation, or abandonment. It is very important not to disturb seal colonies during the breeding season as the cows are very sensitive to disturbance and may abandon their young if they feel threatened. The cow stays close to its pup until it is weaned so it doesn't swim out to sea to feed during this time and relies on its fat stores instead.

During the breeding season, bulls compete for territory and access to females. They often fight each other and the strongest establish territories where they can attract a number of females. Very large bulls can defend large territories and may attract a 'harem' of up to 10 cows. These large bulls with the best territories are sometimes called 'beachmasters'. Because bulls must always defend their territories, they are afraid to leave to go hunting out at sea, so they don't eat for about eight weeks. Instead, they must live off their stored body fat during this time.

After mating, females usually leave the colony. Due to a special delay in their breeding cycle, they do not become pregnant properly for several months. The fertilised egg stops developing so that the pup will be born at a suitable time the following year. Proper pregnancy lasts for about eight months before the cows return to their traditional breeding site. Cows start to breed at about four years old, and may live to over 40. Bulls are fully grown when they are about six, but are better able to defend territories when they are about 10 years of age, so this is when they succeed in breeding. Bulls live for up to 25 years.

Plastic diving fins help the human to swim. The legs of seals, such as this grey seal have developed into special flippers. Seals spend most of their time in the world's seas, so we call them 'marine mammals'.

A Common/Harbour Seal basks in the sun.

Common/Harbour Seal

Rón breacach (beag)
Phoca vitulina

Length: Bull 1.5m;
cow 1.4m
Weight: Bull 90kg;
cow 75kg

Despite its name, the 'common' seal, Phoca vitulina, is less common today in Ireland than the grey seal. It is also known as the 'harbour seal'. The male is called a 'bull', the female a 'cow', and young are called 'pups'. If you go out looking for seals around the Irish coast and our islands, you may come across large groups of seals basking in the sun among rocks or on a sandbank. Despite appearances, common seals do not live in groups or 'herds' like grey seals do. They are also less noisy and less aggressive than grey seals.

Common seals vary in colour from beige to dark grey, with dark spots all over the body. Compared with the grey seal (the other seal found around the Irish coast), the common seal has a round face, a short muzzle and its nostrils form a V-shape. The grey seal's nostrils are more parallel. When wet, common seals look almost black and very sleek. Bulls are larger and usually darker in colour than cows. Adults moult their coats between late August and September.

Diet
The common seal feeds on fish mainly found near the sea bed, such as flatfish, sandeels, whiting, and herring. It also eats squid, molluscs and crustaceans. Young pups feed on shrimps and crabs for a few months after they are weaned.

The common seal pup is born with the waterproof fur and blubber that will provide insulation under water, so it starts to swim almost from birth.

The common seal is often seen basking on rocks or sand banks. Common seals vary in colour from beige to dark grey, with dark spots

Breeding

Breeding occurs at sea between mid-August and early October. Mating usually takes place in shallow waters. In seals, the young do not form straight away after mating. Instead, a small ball of cells called the 'blastocyst' forms and stays this size for a few months. Due to this 'delayed implantation' and development, the cow enters true pregnancy after two or three months, usually in October. About nine months later, in June or July, a single pup is born in shallow waters or on land.

Breeding colonies, where seals gather to mate and to have their pups, are usually found in estuaries, sheltered beaches, on sandbanks and sea-loughs. The pup is born with the waterproof fur and blubber that will provide insulation under water, so it starts to swim almost from birth. The cow feeds her pup both in water and on land, and it will be weaned by late July when it is about one month old. After the pups are weaned, adults will mate again. Male common seals become mature at about six years of age, females at three or four. The common seal may live to be 20-30 years old.

Seals should not be disturbed while they have young pups as it is very important that pups are fed well so they can grow quickly and learn to hunt for themselves. There is also a danger that females might abandon pups if the colony is disturbed by humans.

Simon Ingram

Bottlenose Dolphin

Deilf bolgshrónach
Tursiops truncatus

Length: Males 3.9m; females 3.2m
Weight: Males 270kg; females 190kg

The bottlenose dolphin is the third most frequently observed cetacean around the Irish coast. It is seen regularly off all coasts. It can dive down to 300 metres below the surface of the water.

There is a resident group of bottlenose dolphins in the Shannon Estuary, and they are also recorded in bays and estuaries throughout Ireland, especially in the Irish Sea, Killary Harbour, Dingle Bay, Sligo Bay, Galway Bay and Clew Bay. About 40-

50 bottlenose dolphins spend the whole year in the Shannon Estuary and during the summer the number spotted here may rise to over 100.

Bottlenose dolphins are found in seas all around the globe, and different populations vary in size. Males are slightly longer and heavier than females. They range from grey-brown to dark grey, and their underbelly is white. Young dolphins are called calves.

Diet

The blowhole, through which the dolphin breathes, is on the top of its head. After it takes in air, the bottlenose dolphin can dive under water to hunt for fish for 5-10 minutes or more. Bottlenose dolphins can make lots of different sounds. They use high-frequency clicks to find their prey using echolocation – like bats, they send out sounds and use the returning echoes, as they bounce off objects, to help them locate their prey. This helps them to find fish such as mullet, eels, shad, dogfish, cuttlefish and squid.

Bottlenose dolphins have a varied diet and this is probably why they are found all over the world. They usually hunt fish that live near the sea floor so they are found near land, where the water is not as deep as in the open ocean. Sometimes they hunt alone, but they also hunt in groups, herding fish towards the surface of the water.

The bottlenose dolphin has a very good sense of hearing and good eyesight. As well as sounds used for echolocation, it also makes sounds to communicate with other dolphins. They are very social animals. They usually live in groups of about 15 animals and they will defend their group if threatened.

Breeding

The bottlenose dolphins found in the northern hemisphere breed mainly between May and September and mothers give birth to calves between March and September. The mother dolphin is pregnant for a year and when the calf is born, it is over a metre long. The calf is born tail first so that when it is clear of the mother's body it can swim to the surface straight away to take its first breath. The calf feeds on its mother's milk for between one and three years, and stays close to its mother for up to six years. When it reaches 10 years of age it is a fully-grown adult, and may live to reach 40.

Sometimes dolphins swim with humans. These dolphins must always be respected as they are wild creatures. They are not just endearing, they are also wild animals that hunt prey. This must be remembered.

Bottlenose dolphins often 'breach', jumping clear of the surface of the water. They are also known to ride on the bow wave of boats. They seem to enjoy this as they use less energy than normal swimming.

Bottlenose dolphins
are very social
animals, living
together in
family groups.

Nigel Motyer

Short-beaked Common Dolphin

Deilf/Dorad

Delphinus delphis

Length: Males 2.4m;
females 2.1m
Weight: Males 120kg;
females 75kg

The common dolphin is the second most frequently seen cetacean in Irish waters, and is regularly seen off the south and west coasts. The common dolphin is found all over the world, in the open ocean and in coastal waters. Recently two species of common dolphin have been recognised: the short-beaked and the long-beaked, which is found in the eastern north Pacific. There may be even more species that we once thought were the one species, the common dolphin.

The upper body is brownish black to black in colour and the belly is pale. There are large yellowish patches on each side of the body and long black stripes running to the beak. The blowhole is on the top of the head. Common dolphins produce a range of sounds including clicks and buzzes for echolocation and whistles for communication. They have very good hearing and good eyesight.

Like other dolphins, common dolphins are very social animals, living in groups of up to 25 animals. Groups of hundreds of common dolphins are regularly seen. They work together in many ways, including hunting, and are sometimes seen travelling with other cetaceans.

Diet

Common dolphins feed on fish and can dive to almost 300 metres, for up to eight minutes, in search of prey. They eat sprat, pilchards, whiting, pollock and mackerel, and any other small fish they can catch. They hunt individually and sometimes they cooperate with others to catch prey.

Breeding

Breeding occurs between July and October. In the northern hemisphere, most births take place between June and September, after a gestation period of about 11 months. As with the bottlenose dolphin, it is thought that females support each other during labour. When a mother gives birth to her calf, another female is usually with her. The newborn calf is 80cm in length and will be suckled by its mother for about a year and a half. It becomes an adult at about 6 years of age and may live for 30 years.

Harbour Porpoise

Muc mhara
Phocoena phocoena

Length: Males 1.5m; females 1.7m
Weight: Males 65kg; females 45kg

Maria Archbold

The harbour porpoise's Irish name means 'sea pig' and this is probably because it has a dumpy, stout body and is quite round. It has a thick layer of blubber to provide insulation. It is also sometimes called the 'common' porpoise.

It is the smallest cetacean found around Ireland and is the most frequently observed, particularly in the Irish Sea and off the west coast. Because numbers of harbour porpoises in other parts of Europe are falling, the Irish populations are very important.

The harbour porpoise's upper surface is dark grey, while its sides are lighter and the belly is white. It has a blunt nose, like the larger whales, and the blowhole is on the top of its head. They have excellent hearing and good eyesight and produce a variety of sounds for echolocation and communication.

Diet
The harbour porpoise feeds on herring, mackerel, whiting, flatfish, sandeel, cuttlefish, squid and crustaceans. In Irish waters it is known to eat poor cod, whiting and sprat.

Breeding
Common porpoises are usually seen in small groups of two to 10 animals. Breeding occurs between June and September and most calves are born between May and July, after 11 months' gestation. The calf is about 70cm when born and will be fed by its mother for about eight months. It reaches adulthood at about four years and may live for up to 20 years.

Bottlenose dolphins sometimes attack harbour porpoises. Zoologists do not know why this happens but it may be due to competition for food.

Maria Archbold

Killer Whale

Cráin dubh
Orcinus orca

Length: Male 7-8m
Female: 6-7m

The killer whale is a toothed whale, like the bottlenose dolphin, and is the largest member of the dolphin family, reaching a weight of five tons. The killer whale got its name because it preys on other whales, dolphins, seals and penguins, as well as large fish.

Killer whales use echolocation to navigate and to find prey and they are very fast swimmers, reaching speeds of 55 kilometres per hour. They will follow prey for hundreds of kilometres.

An adult male can measure up to 9.5 metres in length. The large dorsal fin (that is usually seen sticking out of the water from the animal's back, when they surface) can be two metres tall.

Killer whales are regularly seen in small numbers in Irish waters. In June 2001, three killer whales swam up the River Lee in Cork and stayed in Cork Harbour for almost three months, to the great surprise of locals.

The female killer whale starts to breed at 12 years of age and gives birth to a single calf between October and January in the North Atlantic. The calf is fed on the mother's milk for about a year. Male killer whales may live for 50 years, while females may live to 80.

Minke whale

Droimeiteach beag/ Míol mór mince
Balaenoptera acutorostrata

Length: 7-10m
Female: 10-15 tonnes

The minke whale is the most frequently observed baleen whale in Irish waters. They are regularly seen off all our coasts, especially the west coast. It measures up to eight metres in length and weighs about 10 tonnes. The female is a little larger than the male. Its skin is dark grey, brown or black and its belly is white. It has a long pointed snout. The upper fin is quite small and in animals in the northern hemisphere the pectoral fins have a white stripe.

Diet
The minke whale is a 'baleen' whale. Its mouth contains about 600 baleen plates that allow it to sieve huge amounts of water for plankton. They emit special high-pitched sounds and clicks that they use in echolocation to help them find food.

They filter tiny animals from the water called 'krill', and also eat small fish, such as sandeels, cod, herring and small squid. They eat more fish than other baleen whales, who specialise in krill. A minke whale will swim through shoals of fish with its large mouth open to scoop up fish and are also known to chase fish to the surface and herd them into large groups before engulfing them.

Breeding
In the northern hemisphere, breeding usually occurs in February. Pregnancy lasts for about 10 months and calves are born in December or January. The calf is 2.5 metres long at birth. It is fed on its mother's milk for six months and stays close to its mother. The calf will reach maturity at six years of age and may live to be 50 years old.

Humpback whale

Míol mór dronnach
Megaptera novaeangliae

Length: 11-16m

The humpback whale is found all over the world, in all oceans, and is a regular visitor to Irish waters. It is well known for its 'song'. It has the most varied range of sounds of all whales. Some sounds are like long moans; others are like whistles, clicks and chirps. It is the male that produces the 'songs', long series of sounds that are repeated back and forth from animal to animal. The males may use these songs to attract females and warn off other males during the breeding season. Scientists believe other whales may be able to hear a male's song from as much as 150 kilometres away.

Despite their large size, humpback whales are very agile and can leap clear out of the water – this is called 'breaching'.

The humpback whale is black or grey and its underside is paler with white patches. Adult males can grow to 15 metres in length and females can be even longer. Adults can weigh 35-40 tonnes.

The flippers on the sides of its body are very long and can grow to about 5 metres in length! Its head is also very large, up to one-third of its body length.

The humpback whale has paired 'blowholes', its nostrils. The expelled air and spray sent up from the blowhole after a dive is called the 'blow'. The blow of the humpback whale can reach three metres in height.

The humpback whale is a 'baleen' whale. Its mouth contains about 400 baleen plates on each side, which have bristles to help it sieve plankton from water, on which it feeds. Humpback whales can stay underwater for up to 30 minutes, before returning to the surface to breathe. Despite their large size, heavy bodies and awkward-looking shape, humpback whales are very agile and can leap clear out of the water – this is called 'breaching'. Breaching may be used to stun or panic shoals of fish under the surface and can also be used to communicate with other members of the herd. They also slap the water surface with their tail and long fins, and do back-flips.

In winter humpback whales migrate from the colder polar regions to breeding areas closer to the equator. This is where they give birth and mate. In summer they return to northern waters. Humpbacks travelling from Iceland to the Carribean for the breeding season pass along the west coast of Ireland.

Diet

Humpback whales usually feed close to land. They swim through a shoal of fish with their mouths open. They take in a huge amount of water this way and it is sieved through their baleen plates and the filtered fish is swallowed. They eat krill, small crustaceans, fish and squid. Humpbacks use a special hunting technique, known as 'bubble netting'. One or two humpbacks swim up below a shoal of fish, while spiralling and blowing bubbles. This causes the fish to swim into the centre of the ring of bubbles, towards the other fish, and so they become concentrated in the centre. As the humpbacks reach the surface, they open their huge mouths and engulf the fish. In this way, working together with another humpback, they are very efficient at hunting shoals of fish.

Like other whales, the humpback whale arches its back before it dives and this is how it got its name, 'humpback'. The dorsal fin is quite small and is found on a hump about two-thirds of the way down its back. This animal was photographed off the west of Cork

Family

Humpback whales are either seen separately or in groups of up to five animals. On feeding grounds or areas where there is plenty of food available in shoals of fish, many humpbacks may be seen together.

In the northern hemisphere mating usually occurs around February. Males can become aggressive when competing for access to females. They will barge into each other and may also compete vocally – by using their song to warn off other males. The calves are born the following year, in January or February. The calf is usually about four metres long and weighs two tonnes when it is born. It is fed by its mother's milk for up to 10 months. A humpback whale can live to about 90 years of age, but most probably only reach their forties.

African
elephant

Man

Blue whale

Harbour porpoise

Common dolphin

Bottlenose dolphin

Minke whale

Killer whale

Humpback whale

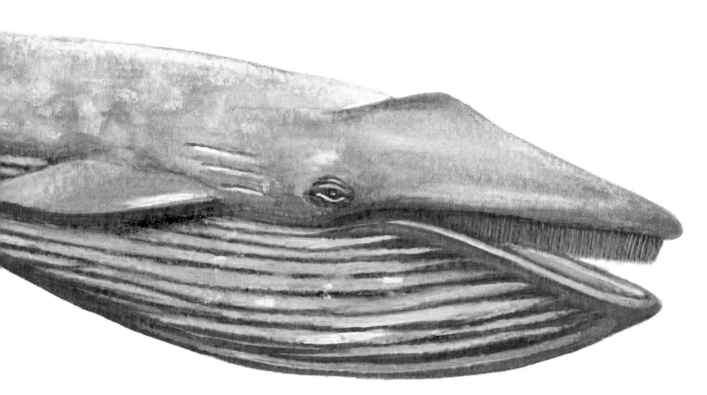

Blue whale

Míol mór gorm
Balaenoptera musculus

Length: 24-27m
Weight: 80-130 tonnes

The blue whale is the largest animal that has ever existed – larger than any dinosaur that ever lived on earth. It is difficult to imagine this animal's size – it weighs about the same as 33 African elephants, the largest land mammal. The Irish name means 'big blue beast'. The largest blue whale ever found measured 33.5 metres! The blue whale calf is seven metres long and weighs about 3,000kg at birth!

The blue whale is a baleen whale. Instead of teeth, baleen whales have baleen plates in their jaws. The blue whale takes in huge amounts of water, which it sieves for small plankton and fish.

Each year, blue whales migrate from their northern feeding grounds to breeding grounds near the equator. This giant used to be a regular visitor to Irish waters. They may be more rare today, but 30-50 blue whales are thought to pass through Irish waters each year.

Other Marine Mammals seen in Irish waters

These three fin whales (*Balaenoptera physalus*) were seen off Cork's coast. Fin whales are regularly sighted around Ireland

Padraig Whooley

Walrus

The walrus (**Rosualt**, *Odobenus rosmarinus*), sometimes visits Irish waters and has been sighted along the west coast. The walrus belongs to the seal family.

Cetaceans:

Some 31 whale and dolphin species are found in European waters, and 24 of these have been recorded in Irish waters, as follows:

Bottlenose dolphin, Deilf bolgshrónach, *Tursiops truncatus*

Common dolphin, Deilf, *Delphinus delphis*

Harbour porpoise, Muc mhara, *Phocoena phocoena*

Killer whale (Orca), Cráin dubh, *Orcinus orca*

Striped dolphin, Deilf riabach, *Stenella caeruleoalba*

White-sided dolphin, Deilf le cliathán bán, *Lagenorhynchus acutus*

White-beaked dolphin, Deilf na ngoba bána, *Lagenorhynchus albirostris*

False killer whale, Cráin dubh bréagach, *Pseudorca crassidens*

Long-finned pilot whale, Míol phíolótach, *Globiocephala melaena*

Risso's dolphin, Deilf liath, *Grampus griseus*

Minke whale, Míol mór mince, *Balaenoptera acutorostrata*

Humpback whale, Míol mór dronnach, *Megaptera novaeangliae*

Fin whale, Míol mór eiteach, *Balaenoptera physalus*

Blue whale, Míol mór gorm, *Balaenoptera musculus*

Sei whale, Míol mór an tuaisceart, *Balaenoptera borealis*

Sperm whale, Caisealóid, *Physeter macrocephalus*

Northern bottlenose whale, Míol bolgshrónach, *Hyperoodon ampullatus*

Pygmy sperm whale, Caisealóid beag, *Kogia breviceps*

Beluga, Míol mór bán, *Delphinapterus leucas*

Cuvier's beaked whale, Míol mór le gob gé, *Ziphius cavirostris*

Gervais' beaked whale, Míol mór gobach na h-Eorpa, *Mesoplodon europaeus*

The northern right whale, Fíormhíol mór na Bioscáine, *Eubalaena glacialis*

Sowerby's beaked whale, Míol mór gobach an tuaisceart, *Mesoplodon bidens*

True's beaked whale, Míol mór gobach le clár-fiacla, *Mesoplodon mirus*

Mamaigh na hÉireann

An luch fhéir
Wood mouse

Tá súile agus cluasa móra ag an luch fhéir agus tá sí níos gleoite ná an luch thí. Tá sí níos cleachtaithe ar bheith ina cónaí taobh amuigh i ngach saghas aimsire ná an luch thí. Faightear í i ngairdíní, san fhál, ar fheirmeacha agus i gcoillte. I rith an lae fanann said faoi thalamh ina n-uachaisí ina mhothaíonn siad slán sábháilte. Istoíche tagann siad amach chun bia a aimsiú. Itheann siad síolta, sméara, dearcána, muisriúin agus ainmhithe beaga ar nós seilidí agus péisteanna talún. Gach oíche taistealaíonn an luch fhéir fhireannach limistéar chomh mór le leath pháirc peile ag lorg bia.

An luch rua / Vól bruaigh
Bank vole

Thángthas ar an luch rua don chéad uair in Éirinn sna naoi déag seascaidí. Fuarathas é beo i gCo. Chiarraí agus ó shin tá sé le fáil in áiteanna i Laighean, Mumhain agus chomh fada le Gaillimh. Is cosúil le haimstéir é lena aghaidh bheag agus a chorp gearr.

Tá sé éasca idirdhealú a dhéanamh idir é agus an luch fhéir agus an luch thí de bharr go bhfuil eireaball níos giorra agus súile agus cluasa níos lú ag an luch rua. Faightear an luch rua i gcoillte agus sna fálta. Bíonn said gníomhach de ló is d'oíche, ag bogadh timpeall sa scrobarnach mar a lorgaíonn siad bia.

Itheann siad plandaí, síolta, sméara, fungas, feithidí agus péisteanna. Is dreapadóirí maithe iad agus mar sin tá seans maith ann go bhfeicfear iad ag dreapadh ins na géaga ísle san fhál, má tá an t-ádh leat.

An luch thí
House mouse

Tógadh an luch thí go hÉirinn trí thimpiste ar bord loinge sa seachtú gcéad. Tá cóta liathdhonn ar an luch thí agus eireaball fada. Taitníonn léi a bheith ina cónaí i bhfoirgnimh de dhéantús duine agus is mar gheall ar sin a fhaigheann sí a hainm. Faightear í freisin ina cónaí san fhál agus i bpáirceanna agus taobh istigh faigheann sí go leor teasa agus compórd faoin urlár agus sna ballaí. Cosúil le francaigh faightear iad in aon áit a mbíonn dramhaíl nó bruscar.

Beireann an luch thí idir ceithre agus deich gcoileán suas go deich n-uaire sa bhliain!

An francach donn
Brown rat

Tagann an t-ainm Gaelach 'Francach Donn' ón gcreideamh gur tháinig an francach seo ón iasacht. Tá sé sin fíor. Is dócha go bhfacthas an cineál seo don chéad uair riamh san tSín nó in oirthear na hÁise agus gur leath sé ar fud na hÁise agus go dtí an Eoraip. Is cosúil gur tháinig sé go hÉirinn go luath san ochtú haois déag ar bord long trádála. Bíonn an francach donn go maith chuig an snámh is an dreapadóireacht agus is cinnte go mbíodh sé éasca dó dul i dtír trí dhreapadh anuas rópa nó trí léim ón long a bhíodh ag dul faoi agus ansin snámh i dtír. Tá na francaigh seo coitianta anois ar fud na hÉireann.

Le linn míonna an Earraigh is an tSamhraidh cónaíonn siad go minic lasmuigh in uachaisí, faoin bhfál agus i measc na mbarr. Ansin san Fhómhar, de réir mar a éiríonn an aimsir níos measa, is minic a bhogann siad isteach i seanfhoirgnimh agus monarchanna. Is speiceas an-tábhachtach é an francach donn d'ár n-ainmhithe creiche. Ciallaíonn sé sin go gcoimeádann sionnaigh, éin seilge agus éasóga smacht ar mhéad na bhfrancach a rathaíonn ar ár mbruscar.

An ghráinneog
Hedgehog

Bíonn níos mó ná cúig mhíle dealg ar a droim ag an ngráinneog. Bíonn siadsan an-úsáideach mar nuair a bhíonn sí i ndáinséar cuireann sí cuma liathróide uirthi féin agus cosnaíonn na deilgne í ón gcuid is mó dá naimhde (na hainmhithe creiche).

Bíonn an ghráinneog le fáil sna coillte, sa ghairdín, sa mhóinéar agus san fhál. Bíonn siad níos gníomhaí san oíche. Itheann siad ciaróga, mamaigh bheaga, uibheacha éan, péisteanna, feithidí, seilidí agus fiú ainmhithe marbha a dtagann siad orthu. Itheann siad torthaí agus sméara freisin.

Geimhríonn an ghráinneog – sé sin le rá go gcodlaíonn sí don gheimhreadh. Tagann an t-ainm 'Gráinneog' ón bhfocal 'gránna' ach is dóigh lena lán daoine go bhfuil siad go h-álainn.

An dallóg fhraoigh
Pygmy shrew

Tá súile beaga bídeacha ag an dallóg fhraoigh agus is dócha gur ón tréith sin a dtagann a hainm gaelach. Ciallaíonn 'Dallóg Fhraoigh' ainmhí dall an fhraoigh. Tá pus fada aici agus féasóg leicinn a bhogann mar a lorgaíonn sí trí dhuilleoga le haghaidh bia.

Is í an dallóg fhraoigh an mamach is lú in Éirinn. Ach cé go bhfuil sí beag cosnaíonn sí limistéar an-mhór agus cuireann sí an ruaig ar dhallóga eile. Bíonn siad go han-mhaith chuig dreapadóireacht agus snámh. Itheann siad ciaróga, cláirsigh agus feithidí eile.

An t-iora rua
Red squirrel

Taitníonn leis an Iora rua bheith ina chónaí i gcoillearnach bhuaircíneach, coillte giúise ina measc, áit ar féidir leis go leor síolta cóin, pailin, bachlóga agus péacáin a ithe. Chomh maith leis sin itheann siad cnónna agus dearcána ó chrainn dhuillsilteacha. Caitheann siad a lán ama go hard sna crainn. Úsáideann siad a gcrúba ghéara chun greim a fháil ar an gcoirt agus iad ag dreapadóireacht. Tógann siad neadacha móra ar a dtugtar 'dreys' go hard sna crainn le cipíní agus féar. Bíonn gruaig fhada ar an Iora rua ag barr a chluasa. Ó tháinig an t-Iora Glas go hÉirinn níl an t-Iora rua chomh coitianta sa tír seo is a bhíodh cheana.

An t-iora glas
Grey squirrel

Tagann an t-Iora Glas ó na coillte duillsilteacha in oirthear na Stát Aontaithe agus Ceanada. Scaoileadh roinnt díobh i Longfort i 1911 agus tá an t-ainmhí seo le fáil anseo i bhfiche contae in Éirinn. Dealraíonn sé go mbíonn an t-Iora Glas níos láidre ná an t-Iora Rua agus is féidir leis coimhlint níos fearr a dhéanamh agus mar sin tá sé le fáil in áit an Iora Rua in oirthear na hÉireann.

Uaireanta baineann siad an choirt den chrann chun an sú a fháil. Cuireann siad bia i dtaisce faoin dtalamh don gheimhreadh. Déanann siad dearmad ar an áit ina chuir siad na cróanna. Fásann crainn astu. Is mar sin a chabhraíonn siad le scaipeadh na síolta.

An ialtóg fhad-chluasach
Brown long-eared bat

An bhfeiceann tú cá bhfaigheann an ialtóg seo a hainm? Tá cluasa an-fhada uirthi a bhíonn beagnach ar chomhfhad lena corp. Faightear an ialtóg fhadchluasach dhonn go coitianta ar fud na hÉireann. I rith míonna an tsamhraidh roghnaíonn na baineannaigh poill i gcrainn agus i bhfoirgnimh mar fhara máithreachais. I rith an gheimhridh geimhríonn said in uaimh nó faoi thalamh i mianaigh nó taobh thiar de na tílí i bhfoirgnimh.

Déanann an chuid is mó de na hialtóga fuaimeanna agus úsáideann said a macallaí chun cabhrú leo a gcreach a aimsiú. Ach ní gá don ialtóg fhadchluasach na fuaimeanna seo a dhéanamh go minic mar is féidir léi na fuaimeanna bídeacha a dhéanann na feithidí a chloisteáil lena cluasa. Níl le déanamh aici ach na fuaimeanna a leanúint chun a creach a aimsiú.

De ghnáth seilgeann an ialtóg fhadchluasach dhonn i measc na gcrann taobh istigh de chiliméadar dá fara agus caitheann siad an lá san áit seo.

Ialtóg fheascrach
Ialtóg fheascrach sopránach
Ialtóg Nathusius
Pipistrelle bats

Faightear trí chineál ialtóg fheascrach in Éirinn, an ialtóg fheascrach sopránach, an ialtóg nathusius agus an ialtóg fheascrach. Is iad seo na h-ialtóga is lú atá againn agus tá siad gaolmhar dá chéile. Is í an ialtóg fheascrach an ialtóg is coitianta a fheictear in Éirinn. Cosúil leis an ialtóg fheascrach sopránach, faightear an ialtóg fheascrach ar fud na tíre. Thángthas ar an ialtóg nathusius in áiteanna in oirthear na tíre. De ghnáth déanann an ialtóg fheascrach sopránach agus an ialtóg fheascrach neadacha máithreachais i bhfoirgnimh, i mbearnaí taobh thiar de chláir, i scéimhil i dtithe agus taobh thiar de shlinnte.

Sa gheimhreadh roghnaíonn siad áiteanna a bhíonn tirim agus fionnuar i gcoguasa i mballaí, sna díonta nó i gcrainn chuasacha le haghaidh geimhriú. Seilgeann an ialtóg fheascrach agus an ialtóg fheascrach sopránach i gcoillte, ar fhéarach, aibhneacha agus lochanna. Itheann an ialtóg fheascrach sopránach gar don uisce, áit a n-itheann siad go leor feithidí a chónaíonn san uisce. Feictear iad go minic ag eitilt go híseal thar bharr an uisce ag piocadh suas leamháin agus cuileoga. Itheann siad réimse leathan de fheithidí freisin.

An ialtóg Leisler
Leisler's bat

Feictear an ialtóg Leisler go coitianta is go forleathan ar fud na hÉireann. Is annamh a fheictear iad i dtíortha eile na hEorpa, tá níos mó díbh le feiceáil sa tír seo. Tá sé an-tábhachtach mar sin go gcosnaímid iad.

De ghnáth faireann an ialtóg Leisler i bhfoirgnimh, in áiléir, faoi thílí agus i bpoill i gcrainn. Sa gheimhreadh úsáideann siad poill i gcrainn, bearnaí i mballaí agus uaimheanna faoi thalamh. Is minic a dhéanann siad aistear de dheich gciliméadar ón mbaile chun bia a aimsiú. Seilgeann siad thar páirceanna agus uisce. Itheann siad míoltóga, leamháin agus cuileoga. Toisc go dtosaíonn siad ag ithe go luath um thráthnóna beireann siad ar fheithidí lae.

An ialtóg ghiobach
Whiskered bat

Is ialtóg bheag í an ialtóg ghiobach. Tá a sciatháin, a haghaidh is a cluasa beagnach dubh. Tá fionnadh dorcha mothallach uirthi agus bíonn dath liath ar a bolg. Tagann a hainm gaelach mar sin óna cuma.

Faightear í ar fud na hÉireann. I rith an tsamhraidh farann siad i bhfoirgnimh agus uaireanta i gcrainn. Dreapann siad isteach i mbearnaí beaga faoi thílí, slinnte agus i mballaí. Sa gheimhreadh geimhríonn siad i mianaigh, in uaimheanna agus i dtolláin. Faigheann siad bia ar thalamh feirme, i gcoillte, i ngairdíní agus thar uisce. Beireann siad ar fheithidí agus iad ag eitilt. Bíonn siad an-lúfar agus ar fheabhas chun eitilte. Piocann siad feithidí freisin ón bhfásra nó ón talamh, ar nós cuileoga beaga, damhain alla agus leamhain.

An Ialtóg Natterer
Natterer's Bat

Faightear an ialtóg Natterer ar fud na hÉireann i gcoillte oiriúnacha. Tá a haghaidh bándearg agus tá fionnadh bán ar a hucht agus ar a bolg. I rith an tsamhraidh farann sí i gcrainn agus i sean-fhoirgnimh agus uaireanta faoi sheandhroichead. I rith an gheimhridh, nuair a bhíonn sé an-fhuar, úsáideann siad áiteanna fuara faoi thalamh in uaimheanna, i mianaigh, i dtolláin agus i siléir. Tagann siad amach go déanach sa tráthnóna. Úsáideann sí na scannáin ina heireaball chun cabhrú léi breith ar creach, ag sluaisteáil suas feithidí chun iad a chur ina béal.

Is eitleoirí iontacha iad agus bíonn siad an-lúfar. Is féidir leo breith ar fheithidí agus iad ag eitilt agus is féidir leo feithidí, damhain alla agus péisteanna chabáiste a phiocadh ón bhfásra. Cosúil le hialtóga eile iompreoidh sí feithid mhór ar nós ciaróige nó leamhain ar ais go dtí a fara sula n-íosfaidh sí iad.

An Ialtóg uisce
Daubenton's bat

Tugtar an t-ainm gaelach sin ar an ialtóg seo mar eitlíonn sí go híseal thar uisce agus scimeálann sí feithidí óna uachtar agus ón aer.

Faightear í ar fud na hÉireann. I rith an tsamhraidh farann siad gar don uisce in áiteanna teo i bpoill i gcrainn, i mbearnaí sna clocha i ndroichid agus i bhfoirgnimh gar don uisce. Don gheimhreadh bogann siad faoi thalamh go mianaigh, uaimheanna agus tithe oighir. De ghnáth snámhann siad isteach i gcoguasa chun geimhriú. Tagann siad amach níos déanaí sa tráthnóna ná ialtóga eile. Is ainmhí lúfar tapa í. Greadann sí a sciatháin go tapa mar a sheilgeann sí thar uisce mallghluaiseacht. Ransaíonn sí freisin trí na crainn a bhíonn gar don uisce. Itheann sí míoltóga agus cuileoga beaga eile, cuileoga Bhealtaine agus leamhain.

An Ialtóg chrúshrónach
Lesser horseshoe bat

Fuair an ialtóg a hainm de bharr chruth a sróin, a bhíonn cosúil le crú. Cabhraíonn sé sin leis an ialtóg na fuaimeanna agus a macallaí a úsáideann sí chun bia a aimsiú a chloisteáil.

Faightear an ialtóg chrúshrónach in áiteanna in iarthar na hÉireann, idir Maigh Eo agus Corcaigh. Sa samhradh farann siad i seanfhoirgnimh nach mbaintear úsáid astu, le slinnte ar an díon. Sa gheimhreadh geimhríonn an chuid is mó de na hialtóga crúshrónacha i mianaigh, in uaimheanna, i siléir nó i dtithe oighir. Faigheann siad bia i gcoillte duillsilteacha. Seilgeann siad míoltóga, leamhain agus cuileoga. Beireann siad ar a gcreach agus iad ag eitilt nó piocann siad iad ón bhfásra

An coinín
Rabbit

Bíonn dath liath-donn, buídhonn nó uaireanta fiú dubh ar choiníní fiáine. Bíonn eireaball clúmhach bán le dath dubh ar a bharr ag na coininí.

Tá an coinín níos lú ná an giorria. Tá cluasa agus cosa níos giorra ag an gcoinín freisin. Itheann siad a lán saghas plandaí. Cónaíonn siad i bpéirí nó i ngrúpaí i gcoinicéir (is córas tollán agus tochailte é). De ghnáth déanann na coiníní a gcoinicéir ar imeall na páirce faoin bhfál nó faoi na driseoga mar bíonn siad ábalta gránadh in aice láimhe.

De ghnáth fágann na cioníní a n-uachaisí nuair a éiríonn sé dorcha. Má bhraitheann an coinín dáinséar buaileann sé a chois dheiridh ar an talamh chun rabhadh a thabhairt do na coiníní eile. Nuair a chloiseann na coiníní eile an torann ritheann siad le haghaidh sábháilteacht a n-uachaisí.

An giorria
Irish hare

Neamhchosúil leis an ngiorria in iarthar na hEorpa, ní thagann dath bán ar chóta an ghiorria Éireannaigh sa gheimhreadh. De ghnáth bíonn a chóta dearg/donn sa samhradh ach athraíonn sé go liath/donn i míonna an gheimhridh. Cosúil leis an gcoinín tá súile an ghiorria suite i dtaobh a chinn agus mar sin bíonn réim radharc de bheagnach 360 céim aige. Is féidir leis an ngiorria bogadh go tapa chun éalú óna naimhde. Itheann siad a lán saghas plandaí cosúil le fraoch, luibheanna, aiteann, cíbeanna, caisearbhána agus féar.

I rith an lae ligeann siad a scíthe os cionn talaimh i dtanalachtaí ar a dtugtar 'foirmeacha'. Síolraíonn siad de ghnáth idir Eanáir agus Meán Fómhair agus is minic a throideann na fireannaigh le haghaidh na mbaineannach ag an am seo. Bíonn siad ag ciceáil is ag dornálaíocht lena gcosa tosaigh agus is féidir iad a fheiceáil ag rith i ndiaidh a chéile agus is mar sin a deirtear fuathu "chomh craiceáilte leis an ngiorria Mhárta".

Giorria gallda
Brown hare

Tógadh an giorria gallda go hÉirinn san naoú aois déag agus san bhfichiú aois. Ceaptar go bhfuil siad fós ag maireachtáil in áiteanna cosúil le hArd Mhacha, Tír Eoghain, Fear Manach agus Contae an Dúin. Ní mór taighde a dhéanamh sula mbeidh sé ar eolas againn cé chomh coitianta is atá an giorria gallda in Éirinn. Tá siad i bhfad níos mó ná coiníní. Glaotar patachán ar an ngiorria óg.

An madra uisce / dobharchú
Otter

Tá an madra uisce cleachtaithe ar shaol san uisce. Tá fionnadh an-tiubh ar a chraiceann chun an t-aer a sháinniú agus a chraiceann a choimeád tirim. Cabhraíonn a scamhóga móra leis fanacht faoi uisce níos faide le linn dó bheith ag tumadh. Is féidir leis snámh go héasca tríd an uisce lena lapaí páirt-scamallacha agus a chorp fada.

Tá féasóg leicinn fada ar a aghaidh a chabhraíonn go mór leis bia a aimsiú sa dorchadas nó in uisce dorcha. Feictear madraí uisce sna haibhneacha, sna lochanna agus ar an gcósta.

Itheann siad éisc agus ar an gcósta gráinneoga trá. Tá an madra uisce sa tír seo an-tábhachtach mar i dtíortha eile na hEorpa tá sé imithe mar gheall ar shealgaireachta agus scrios a thimpeallachta.

An broc
Badger

Is mamach oíche é an broc. Tá stríocaí dubha agus bána ar a aghaidh. Tá fionnadh liath ar a dhroim agus tá a bholg dubh. Bíonn sé go han-mhaith chuig an tochailt agus cabhraíonn a chrúba fada ar a chosa leis chun a bhaile, ar a dtugtar brochach, a thochailt. Bíonn a lán seomraí codlata agus tollán sa bhrochach. Déanann siad tógála an-mhór. Bíonn an broc i gcónaí ag cur lena bhaile, ag iarraidh é a fheabhsú, glúin i ndiaidh glúine.

Cónaíonn broic i ngrupaí sóisialta de cheithre nó cúig ainmhí. Tógann said amach an seanleaba agus seanfhéar go rialta agus cuireann said ar ais féar nua. Sa tslí seo coimeádann siad a mbailte glan agus slachtmhar. Itheann siad péisteanna, mamaigh bheaga, torthaí, cnónna, féar agus bia eile.

An madra rua
Fox

Is é an madra rua an t-aon bhall fiáin de chlann na madraí san lá atá inniu ann. Bhíodh an mac tíre ina chónaí sa tír seo ach tá sé imithe anois. Tá fionnadh álainn liath-rua ar an sionnach agus tá fionnadh dubh ar chosa na sionnach fásta, cosúil le 'stocaí'.

Le teacht an gheimhridh éiríonn a fhionnadh níos tibhe agus coimeádann sé an t-ainmhí te san aimsir fhuar. Is fearr leis na sionnaigh bheith ina gcónaí sna coillte ach bíonn siad solúbtha agus cónaíonn siad anois i gcathracha agus i mbailte móra freisin, ar nós Corcaigh agus Baile Atha Cliath.

Is ainmhí oíche é an sionnach. Nuair a éiríonn sé dorcha seilgeann sé lucha agus creimirí agus itheann siad uibheacha éan, ciaróga, péisteanna agus torthaí chomh maith. Tochlaíonn an sionnach baile faoi thalamh ar a dtugtar prochóg nó ithir. Is ann a bheirtear coileáin agus a théann na sionnaigh fásta chun foscadh a fháil sa drochaimsir. Is ainmhí an-chliste é an sionnach. Is féidir leis dreapadh ar chrainn agus léim ar bhallaí arda.

An cat crainn
Pine marten

Caitheann an cat crainn cuid mhaith dá chuid ama ag barr crann. Bíonn sé an-aclaí agus is dreapadóir fíor-mhaith é. Tá cóta dearg-donn air agus cliabh agus scórnach fionnbhán. Cabhraíonn a eireaball fada mothallach leis chun é a chothromú agus é ag léim ó chraobh go craobh.

Beireann sé greim ar an gcoirt ar na crainn leis na crúba fada géara ar a chosa móra. Bíonn sé gnóthach san oíche ach cúthail i rith an lae. Itheann sé éin, mamaigh bheaga, sméara, muisriúin agus feithidí.

An éasóg
Stoat

Tá corp fada tanaí ag an éasóg. Tá dath donn ar a cóta agus bán ar a bolg, agus tá barr a heireabaill dubh. Tá an éasóg Éireannach difriúil ó na héasóga a fhaightear i dtíortha eile – ní athraíonn a cóta go bán sa gheimhreadh agus bíonn patrún difriúil ar a cóta.

Is féidir leis an éasóg bogadh / fáisceadh trí spásanna bídeacha. Seilgeann sí creimirí, coiníní, éisc, agus éin agus itheann sí uibheacha éan agus feithidí. Cé go mbíonn cosa gearra aici, is féidir léi rith go tapa agus ainmhithe níos mó ná í féin a mharú, ar nós coiníní.

Faightear éasóga san fhál, i gcoillte, sa riasc agus ar thalamh ard. Déanann sí prochóg i gcrainn chuasacha, i mbearnaí i gcarraigeacha agus in uachaisí choiníní.

An mhinc Mheiriceánach
American Mink

Síolraíonn minceanna fiáine in Éirinn ó ainmhithe a d'éalaigh ó fheirmeacha fionnaidh san bhfichiú aois. Faightear iad ar fud na tíre anois. Tá corp tanaí agus eireaball fada aici agus lapaí páirt-scamallacha, a chabhraíonn léi agus í ag snámh.

Cé gur minic a cheaptar gur madra uisce í an mhinc, ós rud é go gcaitheann sí an-chuid ama in aice uisce, tá sí i bhfad níos lú ná an madra uisce agus tá pus rinneach uirthi.

Faightear minceanna ag aibhneacha, sruthanna, lochanna agus ar an gcósta. Déanann said a bprochóga i seanuachaisí choiníní, i gcrainn chuasacha agus uaireanta i seanfhoirgnimh. Itheann siad éisc, coiníní, creimirí, feithidí, froganna agus éanlaith fionnuisce.

An fia rua
Red deer

Is é an fia rua an fia fiáin is mó in Éirinn agus is é ár mamach dúchasach is mó inniu freisin. Athraíonn dath a chóta i rith na bliana. Sa gheimhreadh bíonn dath liath/donn air. Sa samhradh bíonn sé rua. Tá eireaball an-ghearr ar an bhfia. Lasmuigh den séasúr síolraithe cónaíonn na fianna rua i dtréad scartha de bhaineannaigh agus fireannaigh. Bíonn said níos gnóthaí san oíche, ag caitheamh an cuid is mó den lá ag ligean a scíthe.

San séasúr síolraithe idir deireadh Mheán Fómhair agus mí na Samhna, fásann moing ar an bpoc (fia fireann) timpeall a mhuiní. Bíonn beanna móra ar an bpoc. Titeann siad uair sa bhliain san earrach. Díreach tar éis sin tosaíonn beanna nua ag fás agus i mí Lúnasa bíonn said fásta go hiomlán.

I rith an tséasúir shíolraithe déanann na fianna fireannacha coimhlint le haghaidh na mbaineannach trí bheith ag iomrascáil lena n-adharcanna chun a neart a thástáil. Itheann an fia rua duilleoga, féar, torthaí, dearcána, luibheanna agus péacána.

An fia buí
Fallow deer

Faightear fianna buí go fairsing sa tír seo. Tógadh go dtí an tír seo iad don chéad uair leis na Normannaigh. Tá stríocaí dorcha ar a dhroim agus de ghnáth spotaí bána ar a thaobh agus paitse bán. Tá eireaball níos faide air ná mar atá ar an bhfia rua ná an fia Seapánach.

Bíonn beanna leathan ar na fianna fireanna. Is minic a bhailíonn siad i dtréada móra. Cónaíonn na fireannaigh agus na baineannaigh i ngrupaí scartha go dtí an séasúr síolraithe. Bíonn siad gníomhach san oíche. Itheann siad luibheanna, torthaí agus duilleoga freisin.

An fia Seapánach
Sika deer

Is é an fia Seapánach an fia is lú in Éirinn. Ní bhíonn beanna ach ar na fireannaigh amháin agus bíonn na baineannaigh níos lú ná na fireannaigh. Sa samhradh bíonn a chóta donn le stríoca dubh ar a dhroim agus spotaí bána ar an dá thaobh den stríoca. Sa gheimhreadh éiríonn an cóta níos dorcha, liath go dubh.

Cónaíonn na baineannaigh is na hainmhithe óga le chéile i dtréada ach cónaíonn na fireannaigh leo féin. Tagann siad le chéile sa séasúr síolraithe idir deireadh mhí Lúnasa agus tús mhí na Nollag.

Déanann na fireannaigh coimhlint le haghaidh na mbaineannach trí bheith ag iomrascáil lena n-adharcanna chun a neart a thástáil. De ghnáth bíonn na fianna ag innilt go luath ar maidin agus go déanach san tráthnóna. Itheann siad duilleoga, luibheanna, péacána, torthaí, féar, arbhar agus barraí.

An gabhar fiáin
Feral goat

Is ainmhí fiosrach agus neamhspleách é an gabhar fiáin. Seans gur ceansaíodh iad timpeall naoi míle bliain ó shin sa Mheán Oirthear ach ní thógann ró-fhada dóibh éirí fiáin arís má fhágtar leo féin iad.

Itheann gabhair rud ar bith, ina measc plandaí, luibheanna, fraoch agus cíbeanna. Is féidir leo maireachtáil i ngach saghas aimsire. Mar sin éiríonn go maith leo in áiteanna iargúlta ar na sléibhte in Éirinn.

Bíonn píosa spúinseáil faoina chrúba ag an ngabhar agus cabhraíonn sé leis agus é ag iarraidh é féin a chothromú ar na carraigeacha ar na sléibhte. Bíonn adharcanna ar na pocáin agus na minsigh.

An rón mór
Grey seal

Is é an rón mór an rón is comómta a fhaightear timpeall chósta na hÉireann. Déanann siad a lán torainn - tafann, éagaoin, tormáil, siosarnach. Bíonn an bhó níos lú agus níos mílithí ná an tarbh.

Tá an rón mór níos mó ná an rón breacach. Tá ceann cothrom agus polláirí comhthreomhaire air.

I mí Lúnasa agus i Meán Fómhair bailíonn siad le chéile i dtír i ngrupaí móra. Tagann na baineannaigh a bhíonn torrach i dtír chun coileáin a bhreith. Tagann na fireannaigh mar bíonn an séasúr síolraithe ar tí tosú. Beireann an bhó coileán amháin agus cothaíonn sí é ar a bainne ar feadh trí sheachtaine. Bíonn an coileán clúdaithe i bhfionnadh bán go dtí go mbíonn sé trí sheachtain d'aois, nuair a fhásann fionnadh fionnbhán ina áit.

Itheann siad éisc ar nós bradán, scadán, faoitín, leadhbóg, eascainní agus trosc. Téann siad sa tóir ar rud ar bith a bhíonn ar fáil agus itheann siad éanlaith farraige, máthair shúigh agus crústacha freisin.

An rón breacach (beag)
Common/Harbour seal

Síolraíonn dhá chineál róin ar fud na hÉireann - an rón breacach agus an rón mór. Tá brat tiubh blonaig orthu faoina gcraiceann a choimeádann na rónta te. Chomh maith le sin tá brat tiubh fionnaidh orthu atá clúdaithe le hola ó fhaireoga speisialta sa chraiceann. Cruthaíonn sé sin bac leis an uisce timpeall orthu agus coimeádann sé craiceann na rónta tirim.

In ainneoin a ainm as Béarla ní fhaightear an rón breacach chomh comónta is a fhaightear an rón mór. I gcomparáid leis an rón mór bíonn aghaidh cruinn agus puslach gearr air agus déanann a pholláirí cruth 'V'. Bíonn polláirí an róin mhóir níos comhthreomhaire. Síolraíonn siad ar muir idir mí Lúnasa agus tús mhí Dheireadh Fómhair. I Meitheamh nó i mí Iúil beirtear coileán amháin in uisce éadomhain nó i dtír.

Itheann siad éisc a fhaightear gar do ghrinneall na farraige mar shampla scadán, faoitín, máthair shúigh, moilisc nó leadhbóg.

An dheilf bholgshrónach
Bottlenose dolphin

Feictear an dheilf bholgshrónach go rialta ó chósta iarthair agus deiscirt na hÉireann. Tá dath liathdhonn nó dorcha uirthi agus bíonn a bolg bán. Tar éis aer a análú isteach is féidir leis an dheilf bholgshrónach tumadh faoi uisce ag lorg éisc ar feadh deich nóiméad agus níos faide. Déanann siad a lán fuaimeanna agus úsáideann siad a macallaí chun bia a aimsiú. Cabhraíonn sé sin leo chun éisc a fháil, ar nós máthair shúigh, eascainní, cudal agus pincíní. De ghnáth seilgeann siad éisc a chónaíonn gar do ghrinneall na farraige agus mar sin seilgeann siad gar don chosta. Uaireanta seilgeann an dheilf bholgshrónach ina h-aonar ach seilgeann siad i ngrupaí freisin, ag aoiriú éisc chuig barr an uisce.

Tá an t-ainmhí seo an-éirimiúil. Chomh maith leis na fuaimeanna agus na macallaí a dhéanann siad chun bia a aimsiú, úsáideann siad fuaimeanna chun cumarsáid a dhéanamh leis na deilfeanna eile. Bíonn siad an-shóisialta agus de ghnáth cónaíonn siad i ngrupaí. Cosnaíonn siad a ngrupaí roimh bhagairt. Tugann siad aire freisin do laonna na mball eile dá ngrupaí fad is a bhíonn siad ag seilg.

Beireann an mháthair lao idir Márta agus Meán Fómhair. Bíonn an lao nua 1.1 mhéadar ar fhaid. Cothaítear an lao ar bhainne a mháthar ar feadh idir bliain amháin agus trí bhliana agus fanann sé gar dá mháthair suas go dtí sé bhliana.

An dheilf / dorad
Short-beaked common dolphin

Feictear an dheilf go rialta ó chósta iarthair agus deiscirt na hÉireann. Déanann siad réimse leathan de fhuaimeanna, ina measc smeacha agus dorda agus úsáideann siad a macallaí chun creach a aimsiú. Ligeann siad fead freisin le haghaidh cumarsáide.

Itheann siad éisc agus is féidir leo tumadh go dtí beagnach trí chéad méadar ar feadh ocht nóiméad ag lorg bia. Itheann siad faoitín, pliséir, maicréil agus éisc bheaga. Fiachann siad ina n-aonar agus uaireanta i ngrupaí. Is ainmhithe an-shóisialta iad agus cónaíonn siad i ngrupaí móra. Oibríonn siad le chéile i slite éagsúla, ag fiach le chéile agus ag tabhairt aire do laonna a chéile.

San leathchruinne thuaidh beirtear an chuid is mó de na laonna idir mí an Mheithimh agus Mheán Fómhair. Nuair a bheireann an mháthair an lao, de ghnáth bíonn baineannach eile léi - tugann siad tacaíocht dá chéile ag an am seo. Bíonn an lao nua timpeall seachtó ceintiméadar ar fhaid agus cothaítear é ar a mháthair ar feadh timpeall bliain go leith.

An mhuc mhara
Harbour (Common) porpoise

Séard a chiallaíonn an t-ainm seo sa Ghaeilge ná 'muc na farraige' agus is dócha go dtugtar an t-ainm seo uirthi mar gheall ar a corp gearr téagartha agus bíonn sí an-chruinn. Tá brat tiubh blonaig faoina craiceann uirthi a choimeádann an mhuc mara te. Feictear í go minic timpeall na hÉireann. Ós rud é go bhfuil uimhir na n-ainmhithe seo i gcuid eile den Eoraip ag titim, tá sé an-tábhachtach go gcosnaímid na muca mhara a fhaightear timpeall na hÉireann.

Itheann an mhuc mhara trosc, scadán, maicréal, leadhbóga, faoitín, máthair shúigh, crústacha agus rudaí eile. Feictear iad de ghnáth i ngrupaí beaga, idir dhá agus deich n-ainmhí. Beirtear an chuid is mó de na laonna idir Bealtaine agus Iúil. Bíonn an lao nua timpeall seachtó ceintiméadar ar fhaid agus cothaíonn a mháthair é ar feadh timpeall ocht mí.

An míol mór mince
Minke whale

Is é an míol mór mince an míol mór is coitianta a fheictear san uisce timpeall na hÉireann. Feictear iad go minic ó chósta an Iarthair. De ghnáth bíonn sé ocht méadar ar fhaid agus meánn sé timpeall deich dtonna. Tá an baineannach beagáinín níos mó ná an fireannach. Tá a craiceann liathdubh, donn nó dubh agus tá a bholg bán. Tá pus fada rinneach aige freisin.

Is baleen é an Mince. Tá 600 pláta beaga ina bhéal aige. Criathraíonn sé an t-uisce agus itheann sé an planctan. Déanann siad fuaimeanna callánacha agus cabhraíonn na macallaí leo chun bia a aimsiú. Scagann siad ainmhithe bídeacha ón uisce agus itheann siad éisc bheaga ar nós trosc, scadán agus máthair shúigh. Itheann siad níos mó éisc ná na míolta móra baleen eile. Beirtear lao amháin i mí na Nollag nó i mí Eanáir. Bíonn an lao dhá mhéadar go leith ar fhaid nuair a bheirtear é. Cothaítear é ar bhainne a mháthar ar feadh sé mhí agus fanann sé gar dá mháthair.

The National Parks and Wildlife Service

Ireland's National Parks are open to pedestrian traffic all year round at no cost. Walkers should bring suitable clothing and footwear for the weather conditions and terrain they might encounter. Before their visit, people can contact the information points listed below to seek advice in this regard. If venturing into the mountains or remote areas, people are advised not to go alone and should inform someone of their planned itinerary and time of return.

Novices should accompany experienced mountain walkers to learn essential mountain skills. A mobile phone, fully charged, can be valuable for summoning help in an emergency, but remember that not everywhere in the mountains is within coverage. Bringing sufficient supplies of food and drink to provide for delays and emergencies is important.

The National Parks are places for wild nature, and that is what visitors can expect to encounter there, particularly if they leave the official walks and trails. While Ireland does not have dangerous wild animals, there is plenty of rough and treacherous terrain, including mountain cliffs and corries. The weather can change quickly and visibility can decline to close to zero if clouds come down on the mountains. Those leaving the official walks and trails do so at their own risk.

A charge arises for the use of visitor facilities (e.g. the information, guide and interpretative facilities located at a centre in the Parks). There are visitor facilities in all National Parks, except for the Burren National Park and Ballycroy National Park, County Mayo. Visitor facilities are planned for Ballycroy.

Ballycroy National Park, County Mayo

Lagduff,
Ballycroy,
Co. Mayo
Tel. +353 (0) 98 49996

Burren National Park

2 Riverview,
Corofin,
Co. Clare
Tel. +353 (0) 65 6837166

Connemara National Park

Letterfrack,
Co. Galway
Tel. +353 (0) 95 41054 / 41006
Fax +353 (0) 95 41005
Open:
March, April, May, September, October 10.00-17.30
June, July, August 9.30-18.30
Grounds open all year round.

Glenveagh National Park

Churchill,
Letterkenny,
Co. Donegal
Tel. +353 (0) 74 37090
Fax +353 (0) 74 37072
Open: 17 March - 7 November
Daily 10.00-18.30. Last admission 17.00

Killarney National Park

Muckross,
Killarney,
Co. Kerry
Tel. +353 (0) 64 31440
Fax +353 (0) 64 33926
Pedestrian access to the park all year round
Visitor Centre open:
October - March daily on request
April - September daily 09.00-15.30

Wicklow Mountains National Park

Upper Lake,
Glendalough,
Co. Wicklow
Tel. +353 (0) 404 45425
Fax +353 (0) 404 45710
Information Office open:
May - September daily 10.00-18.00
November - April weekends 10.00-dusk
Contact for Christmas and Easter opening hours
Education Centre:
Open throughout the year for school bookings
Tel. +353 (0) 404 45656
Fax +353 (0) 404 45710
email: educationcentrewicklow@duchas.ie

National Parks & Wildlife Service

Department of the Environment, Heritage and Local Government.   www.npws.ie

National Parks of Ireland

AN ROINN COMHSHAOIL, OIDHREACHTA AGUS RIALTAIS ÁITIÚIL
DEPARTMENT OF THE ENVIRONMENT, HERITAGE AND LOCAL GOVERNMENT

Ballycroy National Park, County Mayo

covers 11,800 hectares of Atlantic blanket bog in the Owenduff / Nephin Beg area of north-west Mayo. Ireland's western blanket bogs are the most important bogs remaining in Western Europe, and north-west Mayo contains some of the best examples of this type of habitat.

Glenveagh National Park

covers 16,958 hectares and lies along the Derryveagh mountains in the north-west of County Donegal. The park consists of mountains, bogs, lakes and woods, and is cut in two by the valleys in Glenveagh. The park also contains aspects of cultural heritage, such as Glenveagh Castle.

Connemara National Park

covers 2,070 hectares consisting of rugged quartzite and schist terrain of north Connemara, stretching from sea level at Letterfrack up the slopes and over some of the peaks of the Twelve Bens mountains. A herd of red deer have been reintroduced to Connemara within the park, and there is also a herd of Connemara ponies.

The Burren National Park

covers 1,673 hectares, which include all of the main habitats typical of the Burren area. These include limestone pavement, hazel scrub, deciduous woodland, lakes, turloughs, springs, fen and limestone grassland. Many of the flowers growing in narrow fissures on the limestone terraces are rare elsewhere and the combination of plants usually found in southern Europe is remarkable.

Wicklow Mountains National Park

covers 17,000 hectares that include the Glendalough valley and the two Nature Reserves located there – Glendalough Wood and Glenealo Valley – as well as the areas of the central uplands, including the internationally important Liffey Head Bog and adjoining lands north-east of the Sally Gap.

Killarney National Park

covers 10,289 hectares and includes the lakes of Killarney and most of the Killarney oakwoods which form the largest remaining area of oakwoods that once covered much of Ireland. A herd of red deer roaming the uplands is the only wild herd of these large mammals of native origin left. The park also includes aspects of cultural heritage such as Muckross House and Ross Castle.

CONTACTS

An Taisce - The National Trust
Tailor's Hall, Back Lane, Dublin 8.
Tel. 01-454 1786
email: info@antaisce.org
www.antaisce.org

Badgerwatch Ireland
A non-profit organisation dedicated to
Badgers and actively involved in Badger
conservation, welfare and badger-watching.
5 Tyrone Ave, Lismore, Larn, Waterford.
Tel. 051-373876
www.badgerwatch.ie

BirdWatch Ireland
The largest and most active voluntary
conservation organisation in Ireland, whose
primary interest is the conservation of wild
birds and their habitats in Ireland.
Rockingham House, Newcastle, Co Wicklow.
Tel. 01-2819878
email: info@birdwatchireland.org
www.birdwatchireland.ie

Butterfly Conservation
A non-profit organisation dedicated to
saving butterflies, moths and their habitats.
www.bcni.org.uk

Bat Conservation Ireland
An organisation dedicated to the
conservation of bats.
Batline: 046-9242882   email:
membership@batconservationireland.org
www.batconservationireland.org

Coastwatch Europe Network
Aims include the protection and sustainable
use of our coastal resources and informed
public participation in environmental
planning and management.
Civil & Environmental Engineering,
Trinity College Dublin, Dublin 2.
Tel. 055-25 843 email: dubsky@iol.ie

Conservation Volunteers (Ireland)
Provides practical opportunities for groups
and individuals to protect and enhance our
natural and cultural heritage through
projects, training courses and education.
Steward's House, Rathfarnham Castle,
Dublin 14. Tel. 01-495 2878
email: info@cvi.ie
www.cvi.ie

Conservation Volunteers (NI)
Creates practical conservation opportunities
in the natural and cultural heritage of
Northern Ireland. Beech House, 159,
Ravenhill Road, Belfast, BT6 OBP.
Tel: (028) 9064 5169,
www.cvni.org   email: cvni@btcv.org.uk

Crann
An NGO founded in 1986 to increase the
broadleaf tree cover in Ireland and to
promote/develop Irish broadleaf resources.
Tel. 0509-51 718
email: info@crann.ie
www.crann.ie

Irish Deer Society
Frank Brophy, Chairman, Marne, Ballyhabeg,
Curracloe, Co. Wexford.
Tel. 053-37155
www.irishdeersociety.com

Friends of the Earth Ireland
Plays a constructive role in international
lobbying and campaigning on urgent
environmental and social issues.
22 Sth. Great George's St, Dublin 2.
email: info@foe.ie
www.foe.ie

ENFO
17 St. Andrew's St., Dublin 2
Tel. 1890-200191 / 01-888 2001
email: info@enfo.ie   www.enfo.ie

Forest Friends Ireland – Cairde na Coille
A charity that aims to preserve our native
woodlands and ensure that native trees are
planted in preference to monocultures of
non-native exotics.
PO Box 7814, Dublin 1.
email: info@cairdenacoille.org
www.cairdenacoille.org

Friends of the Irish Environment
A network created by conservationists in
Ireland in order to monitor the full
implementation of European environmental
law, to work for changes in the Irish planning
laws, and to pursue concerns and cases in
both the built and the natural environment
based on the principles of sustainable
community development.
www.friendsoftheirishenvironment.org

Genetic Heritage Ireland
A registered charity that aims to conserve
Ireland's natural genetic resources.
c/o Trinity College Botanic Gardens,
Palmerstown Park, Dartry, Dublin 6
email: geneticheritageireland@yahoo.ie

Groundwork
Workcamps concentrating on
Rhododendron clearance in Killarney &
Glenveagh National Parks.
Groundwork, Sigmund Business Centre, 93A
Lagan Rd, Dublin Industrial Estate, Glasnevin,
Dublin 11. Tel. 01-8602839
www.groundwork.ie

The Heritage Council
The Heritage Council works to protect
and enhance the richness, quality and
diversity of our national heritage for
everyone.
Rothe House, Parliament St, Kilkenny,
Co. Kilkenny.
Tel. 056-7770777
email: mail@heritagecouncil.com
www.heritagecouncil.ie

Irish Peatland Conservation Council
Aims to conserve a representative sample
of living intact Irish bogs and peatlands for
the benefit of the people of Ireland, and
to safeguard wildlife diversity.
Bog of Allen Nature Centre, Lullymore,
Co. Kildare.
Tel. 045-860133
email: bogs@ipcc.ie
www.ipcc.ie

Irish Seal Sanctuary
Ireland's full-time wildlife hospital, rescue
and rehabilitation facility.
Tobergregan, Garristown, Co Dublin.
Tel. 01-8354370
www.irishsealsanctuary.com

Irish Seed Savers Association
An organisation involved in location and
preservation of traditional varieties of fruit
and vegetables.
Capparoe, Scariff, Co. Clare
Tel. 061-921866
www.irishseedsavers.ie

Irish Whale and Dolphin Group
An all-Ireland organisation dedicated to
the conservation and better
understanding of cetaceans (whales and
dolphins) in Irish waters, through study,
education and interpretation. The IWDG
runs the Irish cetacean sightings and
stranding scheme, and the public has
access to the IWDG's database of over
6,500 validated sightings through their
website, www.iwdg.ie. email:
enquiries@iwdg.ie or telephone 023-
31911 for more information on their
work and how you can become involved.

Irish Wildlife Trust
Aims to conserve Ireland's wildlife and
habitats by campaigning, education and
practical conservation.
Sigmund Business Centre, 93A Lagan Rd,
Dublin Industrial Estate, Glasnevin, Dublin
11.
Tel. 01-8602839
email: enquiries@iwt.ie
www.iwt.ie

Mammal, Amphibian and Reptile Society
Northern Ireland, c/o Ulster Museum, Botanic Gardens, Belfast, Northern Ireland.

National Environmental Education Centre NEEC, Knocksink Wood National Nature Reserve, Enniskerry, Co. Wicklow
Tel. 01-286 6609 email: neec@eircom.net

National Parks & Wildlife Service
Department of the Environment, Heritage and Local Government,
7 Ely Place, Dublin 2
Tel. 1890-474 847 www.npws.ie

National Trust, Northern Ireland
Registered charity managing countryside for the benefit of flora and fauna.
email: enquiries@nationaltrust.org.uk
www.nationaltrust.org.uk

Native Woodland Trust
Group dealing with protection, preservation and expansion of Ireland's existing ancient and semi-natural woodlands. email: info@nativewoodtrust.ie
www.nativewoodtrust.ie

Natural History Museum
Merrion Street, Dublin 2
Tel. 01-677 7444
email: naturalhistory@museum.ie
www.museum.ie/naturalhistory/

Tree Council of Ireland
Ireland's umbrella organisation linking together all state agencies, corporate bodies and environmental groups associated with trees and their welfare.
Cabinteely House, The Park, Cabinteely, Dublin 18. Tel. 01-284 9211
email: trees@treecouncil.ie
www.treecouncil.ie

RSPB
The Royal Society for the Protection of Birds works for the conservation of biodiversity, especially wild birds and their habitats.
Belvoir Park Forest, Belfast, BT8 4QT
Tel. (028) 9049 1547
email: rspbnireland@rspb.org.uk
www.rspb.org.uk

Ulster Wildlife Trust
UWT is working to conserve the natural habitats of Northern Ireland by promoting a wider understanding of wildlife issues through communication, education and training and by protecting

species and habitats, both common and rare, and managing 26 nature reserves.
3 New Line, Crossgar,
Downpatrick BT30 9EP
Tel. 028-4483 0282
www.ulsterwildlifetrust.org

The Vincent Wildlife Trust
The Vincent Wildlife Trust is a charity that has been involved in wildlife research and conservation since 1975.
email: vwt@vwt.org.uk
www.vwt.org.uk

Wildfowl & Wetlands Trust Northern Ireland
WWT's mission is to conserve wetlands and their biodiversity.
email: castleespie@wwt.org.uk
www.wwt.org.uk

WWF Northern Ireland
The mission of WWF is to stop the degradation of the planet's natural environment and to build a future in which humans live in harmony with nature.
13 West Street, Carrickfergus,
Co Antrim BT38 7AR
Tel. 028-9335 5166
www.wwf.org.uk

Woodlands of Ireland
Conservation project encouraging appropriate management and creation of native woodlands.
Woodlands of Ireland,
c/o The Tree Council of Ireland,
Cabinteely House,
The Park, Cabinteely,
Dublin 18.
Tel. 01-284 9329
email: woodsofireland@iol.ie
www.woodlandsofireland.com

The Woodland Trust
Conservation charity committed to the protection and enhancement of our native woodland heritage.
1 Dufferin Court, Dufferin Avenue, Bangor, Co. Down BT20 3BX.
Tel. 028-91 275787,
www.woodland-trust.org.uk

Voice of Irish Concern for the Environment (VOICE)
Independent environmental organisation committed to promoting positive solutions to environmentally-destructive activities.
9 Upper Mount St, Dublin 2
Tel. 01-6425741
Email: avoice@iol.ie
www.voice.buz.org

Animal Welfare:

Compassion in World Farming- Ireland
Salmon Weir, Hanover Street, Cork City.
Tel. (021) 427 2441,
email: info@ciwf.ie, www.ciwf.ie

The Donkey Sanctuary
Aims to prevent the suffering of donkeys through the provision of high quality professional advice, training and support. A permanent sanctuary is provided to any donkey in need of refuge.
Knockardbane, Liscarroll, Mallow, Co. Cork
Tel. 022-483 98, email: donkey@indigo.ie
www.thedonkeysanctuary.ie

Dublin Society for the Prevention of Cruelty to Animals (DSPCA)
Ireland's largest animal welfare organisation. A registered charity, established in 1840 to prevent cruelty to animals.
Mt Venus Rd, Rathfarnham,
Dublin 16.
Tel. 01-493 5502/4
email: dspca@eircom.net, www.dspca.ie

The Irish Blue Cross
This 100-year old organisation has a horse ambulance, as well as veterinary mobile clinics for small animals throughout the Dublin area.
Tel. 01-4163030
email: info@bluecross.ie
www.irishbluecross.ie

Irish Society for the Prevention of Cruelty to Animals
The aim of the ISPCA is to prevent cruelty to animals, to promote animal welfare, and to relieve animal suffering.
National Animal Centre, Derryglogher Lodge, Keenagh, Co Longford.
Tel. 043-25035
www.ispca.ie, email: info@ispca.ie

The Monkey Sanctuary Ireland
Ireland's only sanctuary for unwanted monkeys. C/O 25 Bayview Crescent, Killiney, Co. Dublin.
Tel. 01-288 0076
email: yvonne@monkeysanctuary.com
www.monkeysanctuary.com

TACT Wildlife Centre
Talnotry Avian Care Trust, a voluntary charity caring for bird and mammal species.
TACT Wildlife Centre, 2 Crumlin Road, Crumlin,
Co. Antrim, BT29 4AD
Tel. (028) 9442 2900
www.tactwildlifecentre.org.uk

PHOTOGRAPHERS

Mike Brown

As a professional photographer since 1992, Mike has covered many aspects of photography but his first love was always nature. His wildlife photography came to public attention in 2002 when he published his highly acclaimed book, *Ireland's Wildlife – a Photographic Essay*. Mike now runs his own gallery in Clonakilty, Co Cork, where a large selection of his work is available. Tel. 086-8295039 www.mikebrownphotography.com

Eddie Dunne

Eddie has had a lifelong interest in wildlife. He is now very involved in many aspects of photography, including plants, animals, insects and underwater photography, both marine and freshwater. Eddie supplies many photographs for magazines, books, reports and brochures.

Tel. 087-2352169
email: epphoto2003@yahoo.com

John Carey

My love of nature photography, believe it or not, came from my love of hunting, initially with my father. Then as I got older, I got into wildfowling. I soon lost interest and found I wanted more from the beauty of nature and did not want to destroy it. I bought my first camera and lens 20 years ago and have been obsessed ever since. I try to express my photographs as an art form as well as a study in natural history. Tel. 087-7547685

Simon Ingram

Dr Simon Ingram is a cetacean biologist particularly motivated by the ecology and conservation of marine mammals and has worked on marine mammals around the world. Since completing his PhD studies on the ecology of bottlenose dolphins in the Shannon estuary, he has continued to work on marine mammal projects on the west coast of Ireland. Simon is a staff member at University College Cork.

Billy Clarke

Billy Clarke has been a wildlife photographer since the early1980s. "Originally my photography was purely to generate images that could be used as subject matter to paint, but lately photography has taken over." Billy has had photographs and paintings published in many books and magazines. *Exploring Irish Mammals* and two bird guides have been completely illustrated by Billy. Tel. 087-2819386 email: William.Clarke@ucd.ie

Conor Kelleher

Conor's major interest is in bats and he has studied these animals in the field for many years. He has served as Secretary of the UK Bat Conservation Trust and is currently the Vice-Chair of Bat Conservation Ireland and Chairman of the Irish Wildlife Trust.

email: conorkelleher@eircom.net
Tel. 021-7339247
087-2980297

Jacquie Cozens

Jacquie Cozens is a wildlife film-maker, with credits on The Discovery Channel, Channel 5 in the UK, and the BBC. Jacquie is based in Dingle where she co-owns a dive centre.
www.divedingle.com
email: info@divedingle.com

Andrew Kelly

Andrew was born and is based in Dublin. In the early 1990s, he took up photography and has combined this with his love of wildlife and the environment. He has travelled extensively around the world photographing wildlife and wild places. He is a regular contributor to several Irish magazines and occasionally gives talks on wildlife photography.
www.akellyphoto.com
Phone: 086-1568987

Vincent McGoldrick

In 1990, I took up photography with a real interest in wildlife. I was fortunate to win an award in the 1991 Wildlife Photographer of the Year competition which gave me great enthusiasm to capture more of our flora and fauna on this lovely island on film. Patience is a great necessity and can pay great dividends. The main challenge is to capture a subject in a different pose or displaying behaviour that shows it in a new perspective.
Mob. 0044-(0) 77954 155 27

Phil Richardson

Phil Richardson has been working with bats since the early 1980s and works on their conservation in the UK and Europe.
Phil has published two books, both called *Bats*.
email: PRichaBat@aol.com

Richard Mills

Richard's lifelong interest in nature began by observing his garden birds and wildlife. Richard has been a press photographer with the Examiner Group since 1967, covering many national and international events. An avid birdwatcher, he is a well-known wildlife photographer and his work has featured in many Irish and international calendars, magazines and books.
Tel. 086-862 3890
email: birdpics@newsguy.com

Philip Smyth

"I have had a lifelong interest in wildlife and photography. About 17 years ago, I joined the Galway Camera Club where my interest in wildlife photography developed into what some would call an obsession. I concentrate on our more common species as I feel their beauty is often taken for granted." Philip has won local and national awards and his work has appeared in many publications. Tel. 091-555814

Nigel Motyer

Nigel Motyer began diving in 1985 and became involved with photography after that. He is an internationally respected photographer having travelled extensively around the globe shooting a variety of subjects. Nigel's work has been published extensively in books and diving publications together with trade and advertising media. In 2003 and 2004 Nigel assisted Brian Skerry in Ireland with a story for *National Geographic*.
email: nigelmotyer@eircom.net
Tel. 087-606 2959

Padraig Whooley

Pádraig Whooley has travelled extensively overseas following his passion for cetaceans (whales, dolphins and porpoises) and is national coordinator of the Irish Whale and Dolphin Group. When not sitting on Ireland's cliff tops and offshore islands observing whales and dolphins passing along the Irish coast, Pádraig is promoting Ireland's wealth of cetacean diversity and has written extensively on the subject.
Tel. 023-31911, www.iwdg.ie

John N. Murphy

I have been birdwatching for the last 25 years and most of my photography is of birds. As an amateur photographer my photos of birds have appeared in Irish, British, European and American birdwatching magazines and scientific papers. I am currently working on a photographic exhibition and hope to publish more of my photographs in local birding guides and publications.
email: jemurphy@esatclear.ie

Christopher J. Wilson

Educated in Africa and England, Chris obtained an Ecology Diploma in 1999. A policeman in London, he retired early and moved to Ireland to further his ornithological interests. In 1991, he was employed by the National Parks and Wildlife Service, as Warden of Ireland's premier Wexford Wildfowl Reserve. He travels widely and lectures on birds and wildlife of Antarctica, Ireland and South Australia and is never happier than when watching birds and wildlife.

Drawings and Irish translation by Maria Archbold

Maria Archbold is a Secondary School Irish teacher and artist from Newbridge, Co. Kildare.

Maria can be contacted through the author.

Other Photographs:

A number of photographs featured in this book were taken by Ray D'arcy, Carrie Crowley, Conor Lenihan, Pat Falvey and Don Wycherley during the filming of the *Wild Trials* series produced by Crossing the Lines Films for RTE.
For more information, please see www.ctlfilms.ie

Where no name is listed, photographs and illustrations are by Juanita Browne, www.irishwildlife.ie

Cover photographs:
Fox © Philip Smyth;
Otter © Billy Clarke;
Red squirrel © Nigel Motyer;
Grey seal © RTE/Don Wycherley;
Bottlenose dolphin © Simon Ingram;
Badger © Billy Clarke;
Irish hare © John Murphy;
Sika deer © Vincent McGoldrick;
Hedgehog © Mike Brown

Other photographs:
Rabbit family p.5 © Richard Mills
Fox cub p. 8 © John Carey

FURTHER READING:

Exploring Irish Mammals. By Tom Hayden and Rory Harrington. Published by Townhouse, Dublin, 2000.

The Encyclopedia of Mammals. Edited by David MacDonald. Published by Oxford University Press, 2001.

The Fauna of Ireland - an introduction to the land vertebrates. By Fergus J. O'Rourke. Published by the Mercier Press, Cork, 1970.

Nature in its Place - the Habitats of Ireland. By Stephen Mills. Published by The Bodley Head, London, 1987.

Ireland's Wild Countryside. By Éamon de Buitléar. Published by Boxtree Limited London, 1993.

Ireland – A Smithsonian Natural History. By Michael Viney. Published by Blackstaff Press, Belfast, 2003.

Fauna Britannica. By Duff Hart-Davis. Published by Weidenfield & Nicolson, 2002.

Complete Irish Wildlife. Paul Sterry. Introduction by Derek Mooney. Published by HarperCollins, 2004.

Mammals of Britain and Europe. By David MacDonald and Priscilla Barrett. Published by Harper Collins, London (1993).

Primary School Curriculum Science: Social, Environmental and Scientific Education. The Stationery Office, Dublin, 1999.

An Irish Beast Book. By James Fairley. Published by Blackstaff Press, Belfast, 1984.

A Basket of Weasels. Written and published by James Fairley, 2001.

The Bats of Britain and Ireland. By H.W. Schofield and A.J. Mitchell-Jones. Published by The Vincent Wildlife Trust, 2003.

Field Guide to the Animals of Britain. Published by the Reader's Digest Association Ltd, London, 1984.

The Badger and Habitat Survey of Ireland. By C.M. Smal. The Stationery Office, Dublin, 1995.

The Blue Planet. Published by BBC Worldwide Limited, 2001.

Whales, Dolphins and Porpoises. By M. Carwardine. Published by Dorling Kindersley, London, 1995.

Irish Whale and Dolphin Group Cetacean Sighting Review (1991-2001) Published by Irish Whale and Dolphin Group.

The Red Fox. By S. Harris and P. White.
Published by The Mammal Society, London, 1994.

The Badger. By Tom Hayden (ed.)
Published by the Royal Irish Academy, Dublin, 1993.

Stoats and Weasels, Polecats and Ferrets. By P. Sleeman.
Published by Whittet, London, 1989.

Habitat Enhancement for Bats – Guidelines for Government Bodies. Donna Mullen. Published by Bat Conservation Group, Tel. 046-9242882

Wildlife. By Don Conroy and Chris Wilson.
Published by Mentor Press, 1997.

Wildlife Quiz and Amazing Facts Book. By Don Conroy and Chris Wilson.
Published by Natural Rapture Ltd, 1999.

Talking Wild – wildlife on the radio. By Éanna Ní Lamhna.
Published by TownHouse, Dublin, 2002.

Wild and Wonderful. By Éanna Ní Lamhna.
Published by TownHouse, Dublin, 2004.

Ireland's Wildlife – A photographic essay. By Mike Brown.
Published by Mike Brown, 2002.

The Animals of Ireland. By Gordon D'Arcy. Published by the Appletree Press Ltd, 1988.

Birds of Ireland. By Gordon D'Arcy. Published by the Appletree Press Ltd, 1986, 1999.

The Complete Guide to Ireland's Birds. By Eric Dempsey and Michael O'Clery.
Published by Gill & Macmillan, 1993, 2002.

Ireland's Marine Life – A world of beauty. Matt Murphy and Susan Murphy (Ed.) Photography Paul Kay. Published by Sherkin Island Marine Station, 1992.

A Beginner's Guide to Ireland's Seashore. Published by Sherkin Island Marine Station Publications.

Ireland's Bird Life – A world of beauty. Matt Murphy and Susan Murphy (Ed.) Photography Richard Mills. Published by Sherkin Island Marine Station Publications, 1994.

Ireland's Freshwaters. By Julian D. Reynolds. Published by The Marine Institute, Dublin, 1998.

Wetlands of Ireland – Distribution, ecology, uses and economic value. Marinus L. Otte (Ed.) Published by University College Dublin Press, 2003.

Celebrating Boglands. Published by the Irish Peatland Conservation Council, 2002.

Wild Plants of the Burren and Aran Islands. By Charles E. Nelson. Published by the Collins Press.

Wild Plants of south-western Ireland. By Charles E. Nelson. Published by Strawberry Tree, Dublin, 2001.

Wild Plants of Connemara and West Mayo. By Charles E. Nelson. Published by Strawberry Tree, Dublin, 2001.

Flora Hibernica – the wild flowers, plants and trees of Ireland. By Jonathan Pilcher & Valerie Hall. Published by the Collins Press, 2001.

Irish Wild Flowers. By Ruth Isabel Ross. Published by Appletree Press Ltd, 1987.

The Irish Wildlife Book. Edited by Fergus O'Gorman. Published by John Coughlan, 1979.

Meetings with Remarkable Trees. By Thomas Pakenham. Published by Weidenfeld & Nicolson Ltd, 1996.

Native Trees & Forests of Ireland. By David Hickie. Published by Gill & Macmillan Ltd, 2002.

Close-up on Insects – A photographer's guide. By Robert Thompson. Published by Guild of Master Craftsman Publications Ltd, 2002.

Irish Indoor Insects – A popular guide. By James P. O'Connor & Patrick Ashe. Published by TownHouse, Dublin, 2000.

The Natural History of Ireland's Dragonflies. By Brian Nelson and Robert Thompson. Published by the National Museums and Galleries of Northern Ireland, 2004.

The Millennium Atlas of Butterflies in Britain and Ireland. Published by Oxford University Press, 2001.

Photographic Guide to the Sea & Shore Life of Britain and North-west Europe. Published by Oxford University Press, 2001.

Dúlra agus Dúchas – our heritage. By Mícheál MacGinneá and Mairéad Ní Nuadháin. Published by the Stationery Office, Dublin, 1979.

BBC Wildlife magazine, www.bbc.co.uk

The Irish Naturalist's Journal. www.habitas.org.uk/inj

Heritage Outlook, the magazine of the Heritage Council, www.heritagecouncil.ie

GLOSSARY

AMPHIBIAN a type of animal that spends part of its lifecycle in water and part on land. Amphibians are cold-blooded vertebrates. Frogs, toads and newts are amphibians.

BEECHMAST the fruit produced by the beech tree.

BLOW the air exhaled from the blowholes of cetaceans, the whales and dolphins. The blow is the cloud of spray produced when a cetacean releases the air from its lungs after a dive.

BLOWHOLE the nostrils of whales and dolphins. The blowhole is a single or double opening on the top of the animal's head.

BLUBBER the layer of insulating fat in marine mammals such as whales, dolphins and seals.

BREEDING SEASON the breeding season of an animal usually refers to the time of the year when it mates.

BREACHING when a whale or dolphin leaps clear of the water.

BROWSER an animal that feeds mainly on the foliage of trees, herbs and bushes.

CARNIVORE an animal that eats meat. Carnivores have long, pointed canine teeth and claws to help them catch prey.

CETACEANS the whales and dolphins.

CLASSIFICATION the grouping together of plants, animals, rocks or other things that have similar characteristics.

COMMUNITY all the animals that live together in a habitat.

COMPETITION the struggle among organisms for a resource that is in short supply, such as food, oxygen, water, space or mates.

COPROPHAGY the eating of faeces.

CARRION flesh of dead animals.

CRUSTACEANS a group of invertebrates covered with a hard shell, including crabs, prawns and lobsters.

DECOMPOSER organisms such as bacteria and fungi that break down the dead remains of organisms into simpler substances and return them to the soil.

DELAYED IMPLANTATION In mammals, a delay between fertilisation of an egg and the subsequent development of an embryo. This delay allows birth to occur when conditions are favourable for raising young.

DIGESTION the process by which large food particles are broken down and made soluble with the help of enzymes and chewing and grinding teeth.

DIURNAL active during daylight.

DREY the nest of a squirrel. Young are born in a maternity drey.

EARTH the underground home of a fox, where the female gives birth to cubs.

ECHOLOCATION the ability of some animals, such as cetaceans and bats, to 'see' objects by emitting sounds and judging the reflections of those sounds as they return to their ears.

ECOLOGY the study of relationships of organisms or groups of organisms to their environments.

ECOSYSTEM a community of organisms and their relationships with each other and their relationships with their living and inanimate environment.

EXCRETION the release of waste materials from an organism.

FAUNA the collective animal life of a country, area, habitat or time period.

FERAL domesticated animals that become wild, and live independently.

FERTILISATION the joining together of male and female reproductive cells to form new life, a new organism of that species.

FLORA the collective plant life of a country, area, habitat or time period.

FLUKES the tail fins of cetaceans.

FOSSIL the remains of an organism, or evidence of it, preserved through time in rock, amber, tar, ice, volcanic ash or peat. The dating of fossils provides evidence for evolution. Fossils have shown us what creatures roamed the earth in the past, such as dinosaurs, and also tell us how animal groups are related and how they have evolved from their ancestors.

FOOD CHAIN the transfer of energy from one organism to another within a habitat or ecosystem. The food chain shows the feeding relationship between organisms. Each link in the chain feeds on, and obtains energy from, the one preceding it, and is in turn eaten by, and provides energy to the one succeeding it. Here is an example of a simple food chain: grain – wood mouse – fox.

FOOD WEB a linked series of food chains.

GENERALIST an animal that has not become specialised for a particular diet or lifestyle.

GESTATION the period between conception (after successful mating of the male and female) and birth of young.

GRAZER an animal that feeds mainly on grasses.

HABITAT the place where an animal normally lives. An animal's habitat provides a particular set of conditions needed for its life. A habitat may be large, for example, a woodland, or small, for example, a branch on a tree.

HAREM a group of two or more females that stay with one male for mating during the breeding season. For example, the male red deer attracts a harem of females, with which it will mate. It defends its harem from other males so that it can father as many young as possible.

HERBIVORE an animal that only eats plants.

HIBERNATION some mammals can survive through cold periods by becoming inactive, conserving energy and lowering their body temperature. e.g. hedgehogs and bats hibernate.

HOLT the underground home of the otter. The otter digs the underground holt into the riverbank. It can have many exit points, both above ground and opening underwater, so that the otter can slip into the water without crossing land. The otter spends much of the day in its holt.

ICE AGE for many thousands of years the earth was covered by ice. These periods of very cold conditions are termed 'ice ages'.

INCISORS large front teeth used as chisels, for gnawing and cutting.

INSECTIVORE an animal that feeds mainly on insects.

INVERTEBRATE an animal without a backbone. Insects, slugs, crustaceans, and spiders lack a backbone and can be described as invertebrates.

KRILL Euphausids, small shrimp that live in the world's oceans. Baleen whales eat krill.

LIFESPAN the period of time from birth to death of an organism.

MAMMAL an animal with a backbone (a vertebrate) that can maintain its own body temperature. Its skin is covered with hair and sweat glands. The female feeds its young with milk produced by special glands called mammary glands. Mammals have a diaphragm, a sheet-like muscle that separates the chest cavity from the abdomen. The diaphragm is used in breathing.
There are three subclasses of living mammals – the Eutheria: the placental mammals, which include man; the Metatheria, the marsupials, for example, kangaroos and wombats; and the Prototheria, the monotremes, for example, spiny ant-eaters and the duck-billed platypus, which lay eggs.

MAMMARY GLAND a gland that produces milk. Mammary glands are only found in mammals, which feed their young in this way.

MATING SEASON mammals usually mate during a particular time each year, called the mating season. This is timed so that the young are born at a time when conditions are most suitable.

MICRO-ORGANISM minute life form, such as single-celled organisms, bacteria and some fungi.

MOLAR TEETH the cheek teeth of animals; used for chewing and grinding.

MOULT the shedding of hair.

NOCTURNAL active mainly after dark.

OMNIVORE an animal that eats both plants and animals as part of a mixed diet.

ORGANISM a living animal, plant, fungus or micro-organism

PLANKTON small animals and plants that live in lakes and oceans. Plankton are found close to the surface of the water.

POD a group or herd of whales or dolphins.

POPULATION the total number of organisms of a particular species within a particular habitat or area.

PREDATOR an animal that hunts and kills other animals for food.

PREY the animals hunted by predators.

REPRODUCTION the formation of new individuals. Mammals reproduce by sexual reproduction, which involves the joining together of two sex cells, from which a new mammal develops.

ROOST a site bats use to sleep during the daytime or in which they hibernate over winter. Maternity roosts are used for giving birth to and rearing young.

RUMINANT a hoofed mammal with a complex digestive system with a number of chambers. One of these, the rumen, contains micro-organisms which help break down cellulose from plant foods. To help speed up this process, a ruminant usually regurgitates its food and rechews it, a process called "chewing the cud". Deer and goats are ruminants.

RUT / RUTTING SEASON term used to refer to the most active period during the breeding season of goats, deer, seals and some whales.

SCAT the faeces of fox, mink, etc.

SPECIES a particular kind of organism. A classification category that groups animals that share many characteristics in common. Males and females of the same species can breed with each other to produce fertile offspring. The common seal is one seal species found around our coasts. The grey seal is another. These are separate 'species' because they cannot breed to produce fertile offspring, and though they are both seals, they have many different characteristics.
Humans all belong to one species, *Homo sapien*. Dogs all belong to one species – *Canis familiaris*. All dog breeds can potentially mate and produce fertile pups, so despite the variety shown in this species, all domestic dogs belong to just one species.

SPRAINT the faeces of the otter

SPYHOPPING when whales or dolphins raise their heads clear of the water to survey their surroundings

SUBSPECIES populations of a species that have been isolated from each other for long enough for physiological and genetic differences to develop, so that they can be distinguished as separate races.

TERRITORY the area defended by an animal or group of animals. Territorial animals will defend territories from other individuals of the same species.

TORPOR Similar to hibernation; some animals can reduce their metabolic rate and body temperature so as to conserve energy for short periods of time.

ULTRASOUND sound that is above the level of human hearing, above approximately 20kHz.

VERTEBRATE a vertebrate is an animal with a spine made of boney parts called vertebrae. The brain is encased in a skull. Amphibians, reptiles, birds mammals and fish are vertebrates.

WEANING a mammal is 'weaned' when it is no longer fed on the milk of its mother.

INDEX